Principal Leadership Behavior and Faculty Trust
Is There a Connection?

by

Dr. Frank DePasquale

RoseDog🐾Books

PITTSBURGH, PENNSYLVANIA 15222

RoseDog Books
701 Smithfield Street
Pittsburgh, PA 15222
Visit our website at *www.rosedogbookstore.com*

ISBN: 978-1-4349-8683-2
eISBN: 978-1-4349-7679-6

ACKNOWLEDGMENTS

To my wife, Diann, and my daughters, Alicia and Antonia.

To Dr. Naftaly Glasman and the Professors of Educational Leadership at the University of California, Santa Barbara.

To the dedicated administration, faculty, staff, students, and parents at the Moorpark Unified School District in Moorpark, California.

To my parents, Frank and Mary.

TABLE OF CONTENTS

List of Figures

List of Tables

List of Appendixes

PREFACE

Education is at a crossroads in America today. It has always been the bedrock of a democracy, and today that bedrock is becoming weaker. I conducted this study in 1996 as part of my Doctoral Program at the University of California, Santa Barbara. In my concluding paragraph, there is a quote that is disturbingly more relevant today than it was fifteen years ago.

It is as follows: "Our public schools seem to be under attack from all quarters, however, the metaphor should not be the military in times of battle. Rather, it should be the family unit taking care of one and others needs, and making sure that their goals are accomplished while maintaining the family values of trust and support."

This book is about that mutual trust and support that must be found in our schools today. The pressures on students, parents, faculty, administration, and community are greater than ever. The core unit of focus has to be the individual school site. That is where success or failure will take place; that is where the bedrock of our democracy will need to continue to flourish if we are to remain a strong nation.

The key to success at a school site is effective teaching and good administrative support. This cannot take place unless there is a mutual trust between the principal and the faculty. The principal in the role of a leader can foster that trust through a set of a specific behaviors. It can be done, as long as people are willing to change their behavior for the good of the school family. It is my hope that this study will give educators the tools to accomplish this important goal.

CHAPTER ONE

INTRODUCTION

"To be trusted is a greater compliment than to be loved"
- George Mac Donald

The public schools in the United States today have been under-going massive restructuring due to problems arising from a society that is in flux. Demographic changes have required the development of new strategies to meet the challenges of students who have increasing special needs in areas such as Limited English Language Proficiency (LEP) and special education. Changes in the social infrastructure (Kozol, 1991) have also increased the number of students who are living below the poverty level, as well as those who exhibit an array of serious health and psychological problems. Kozol notes that schools and cities that he visited in 1964 in some of our urban areas such as Chicago, New York City, Newark, and Boston have declined even more dramatically and that demographic, ethnic, and socioeconomic differences are more pronounced after 30 years of compensatory education funding. Some of the neighborhood schools he visited were dismal places to be:

> In Boston, the press referred to areas like these as 'death zones' a specific reference to the rate of infant death in ghetto neighborhoods. Looking around some of these

schools, where filth and disrepair were worse than anything I had seen in 1964, I often wondered why we would agree to send our children to schools in places no politician, school board president, or business CEO would dream of working. (p. 5)

This scenario is also playing itself in the large urban areas in the State of California. Alarming as this may be, there does not seem to be any major change in providing the needed resources to improve this condition of our public schools. The State Department of Education, in its 1994-95 Annual Report (Schmidt, 1994), documented that in the past decade we have slipped to the bottom 10 states on spending per pupil and have the highest class sizes in the entire nation. California is in the bottom quartile in the ratio of students per computer, students per librarian, and students per nurse. The report also noted that over the past 15 years the number of children living in poverty has risen from 900,000 to 2.2 million.

In addition, the projected enrollment in California public schools for the next 5 years is predicted to rise to 6,400,00 from its current population of 5,200,000. Many of these additional 1,200,000 students will no doubt have special needs. For example, the number of LEP students has doubled this past decade from 487,800 in 1984 to 1,151,000 to what now constitutes 22% of our K-12 student population. An even more dramatic shift has taken place in the student ethnicity over the past two decades. In 1968, the number of students identified as white was 75%, and in 1994 the percentage of white students had declined to 42%.

These demographic changes are being felt most dramatically in the urban districts, but there are indications that these shifts are also occurring in many so-called "wealthier" suburban districts throughout the state. The demographic changes facing California will ultimately change the ethnic and socioeconomic makeup in all communities, including urban, suburban, and rural. The old methods of school governance will no longer meet the needs of our faculty and student populations. Indeed, we are experiencing a "breakpoint" (Land & Jarman, 1992), with changes that are so sharp, continuous, and significant that we can no longer use our old rules of behavior to solve the problems that we now face.

Dealing with this wide range of student needs will require various levels of faculty cooperation and administrative support. For example, a school that has large numbers of LEP students and a shortage of bilingual or English as Second Language teachers will require increased levels of cooperation among faculty, as well as administration, to serve these student needs. There will also be a need for serving the needs of our increasing special education population, which is currently 553,000, or 10% of our student population. As the demands for mainstreaming and full-inclusion of special-needs students into the regular classroom increase, there will be additional demands for working together as a team. Coordination and collaboration will also become increasing important in dealing with outside social welfare and medical facilities as we attempt to deal with the impacts of students living below the poverty level. A teacher can no longer close the door at 8:00 a.m., open it at 3:00 p.m., and expect not to work in some level of collaboration with either faculty or administration at some point in the day.

These new challenges to the public education system will require new ways of thinking and providing services. Larson and LaFasto (1989) have noted that the concept of teams and team-building in organizations has been the key to success in the private sector for dealing with rapid change. Bennis and Nanus (1985) point out that linear thinking and linear information are no match for today's turbulent societal and business climate. When individuals work together in a team, there is collective wealth of knowledge that seems to have a synergistic effect in dealing with the problems at hand. More creative solutions are offered because the same problem is viewed from a variety of perspectives. In other words, the old adage of the whole being greater than the sum of its parts is very true when it comes to collective decisions.

This team-building has also been referred to by such terms as site-based leadership, shared-decision making, site-based management, quality circles, and similar related terms. Currently, stakeholders in school districts such as teachers, administrators, school board members, and parents are realizing the need for the application of this team-building strategy to occur in our public schools in order for them to maintain their effectiveness.

Blase and Kirby (1992) and Glickman (1990) noted that in schools where shared decision making has been implemented successfully, there was a principal who had established or maintained a positive school climate in which this type of collaboration process could occur. This psychological climate, or school climate, has been identified as one of the factors in Edmonds' (1979) model of effective schools. McGregor (1960) recognized this process in organizations by noting that the subtle day-to-day behaviors of a supervisor created what was often referred to as the "psychological climate" of the organization. This day-to-day behavior of the principal, and its effect on school climate, is the focal point of this study.

Hoy, Tarter, and Kottkamp (1991) viewed the climate of a school as a potential means for making schools more productive to the extent to which the school atmosphere promoted openness, colleagueship, professionalism, trust, loyalty, commitment, pride, academic excellence, and cooperation. They postulated that organizational health and mutual trust are significant features of life in schools: "Healthy schools satisfy the Parsonian requirement that goals be achieved and members integrated into the organization. Trust logically seems a key element in both the instrumental and expressive activities of the organization" (p.108).

This was consistent with Ouchi's (1981) Theory Z corporate culture, where commitment, cooperation, teamwork, trust, loyalty, and egalitarianism were basic to the successful organization.

Although it was not the intention of this study to draw a direct correlation between a principal's behavior and student achievement, indirect impacts have been noted in previous studies by Heck, Larsen, and Marcoulides (1990); Hoy, Tarter, and Bliss (1990); and Bossert, Dwyer, Rowan, and Lee (1982). A relationship to student achievement may be indirect to the degree the principal has the ability to create a healthy school climate in which collaboration and teamwork can take place. Larson and LaFasto (1989) found that instruction is more effective when there is a team effort. The group is more problem focused, and instruction is more efficient because of the increased levels of communication and coordination between the faculty and administration. The positive effects of workplace productivity have also been documented by Sullivan (1988), who identified communicating candidly, confronting issues, and using each other's resourcefulness as factors that affect climate and increase the team's likelihood of attaining their mission, goals, and objectives. It is thus apparent that a principal can create a healthy environment where teaching and learning may take place, and potentially effect student achievement.

Statement of the Problem

Today's educational leaders perform in a societal context that is much more complex than in past generations of leaders. More is expected and even less is available in viable resources and support. This decline in resources, coupled with significant demographic changes that find an ever-increasing number of students ill prepared for the demands of a public school setting, seems to negatively impact many of the public schools in California. There are still principals who rise to the occasion and provide the much-needed leadership in these troubled public schools. These principals establish quality schools and directly effect instruction in the classroom. This is accomplished despite at least one theoretical perspective that indicates that the school principalship is inherently an administrative role rather than a role necessarily determined by its connection to education (Glasman, 1984). These effective principals seem to somehow establish a positive work environment in which the goals of the organization can be achieved. In other words, a principal can behave in such a way that there could be an impact on school effectiveness and thus strengthen their connection to the educational process.

What sets these principals apart from those who are not able to establish such a positive work environment? What are these specific principal behaviors that can be identified as having impacts on the school environment? Is there a direct correlation between a positive work environment and certain principal behaviors? What are the elements that create such a positive school environment? These are some of the major questions that this study attempts to answer.

Positive School Climate and Trust

As Ouchi (1981) has noted, a key factor in establishing this positive school environment, or climate, seems to be the development of trust in the leadership of the organization. Hughes (1974) indicates that you cannot have a positive school climate without the level of mutual trust necessary for establishing positive interpersonal relations. Hoy et al. (1990) support this connection, noting that although the concepts of organizational climate and trust are not identical, they are complementary, and consequently interrelated. Teachers identified being trusted by the principal as the most influential behavior of the elementary school principal (Gomez, 1987). The relationship between trust and a healthy school climate is clear and firmly established in the review of the literature.

In order for the leader of any organization to lead effectively, there must be support from those who are to be led. In the case of a school, the principal must have the support of the teachers in order to achieve most goals and objectives for the student population. One way that this cooperation has been accomplished is by involving the teachers in the decision-making process. In describing this collaborative process, Blase and Kirby (1992) noted that such words as "family," "team," "cooperation," and "community" were used repeatedly. Lee, Dedrick, and Smith (1991) also found that the strongest predictor of teacher satisfaction is a sense of community among their peers; teachers felt a sense of satisfaction in their work when they felt comfortable and non-competitive with their colleagues.

The review of the literature has also indicated that there were certain principal behaviors that were related to establishing this positive school climate (Blase & Kirby, 1992; Glickman, 1990; Russell, Mazzarella, White, & Maurer, 1985; Sullivan, 1988). If these behaviors were genuine and consistent, they appeared to have a correlation with increased levels of faculty trust. Parsons (1961) supported this notion by identifying a significant relationship between consistency, or what he termed "behavior pattern maintenance," and the intrinsic elements of trust.

Key Variables: Principal Behaviors and Faculty Trust

In the review of the literature, four general categories of principal behaviors emerged that could potentially effect levels of faculty trust. They included what will be defined as Praising, Buffering, Involving, and Caring behaviors. These were certainly not the only behaviors identified that could effect faculty trust, but they were the core principal behaviors that were most dominant. The brief summary definitions were as follows:

1. Praising Behaviors: These principal behaviors included recognizing faculty members for their contributions to the organization. This praising behavior was usually characterized as being simple and brief, and they were either written or verbal.

2. Buffering Behaviors: These principal behaviors protected teachers from any undue loss of instructional minutes, as well as protection from angry parents or disruptive students. They included minimizing parent, student, and administrative interruptions.

3. Involving Behaviors: These principal behaviors focused on the effort to involve others in the decision-making process, especially when the outcomes of the decisions had a direct effect on the day-to-day activities of those making the decision.

4. Caring Behaviors: These principal behaviors focused on displaying a genuine concern for the welfare of the teacher. There was also a sincere interest shown in the personal lives of teachers.

The concept of Trust was also a key variable in the study and was generally defined as the firm reliance on the integrity, ability, and/or word of a person or a group of persons, to do what they say they are going to do. A thorough treatment and theoretical framework for these principal behaviors, as well as the variable of Trust, is presented in the review of the literature.

Conceptual Framework

The conceptual framework for this research is based on the central assumption found throughout the review of the literature: There does exist a set of behavioral characteristics among principals that is significantly related to levels of faculty trust. Furthermore, there is a linkage between these principal behaviors in providing a school climate in which a team effort can be accomplished. This is consistent with Parsons' (1961) model that describes the need for organizations to have internal solidarity (integration), as well as a distinctive value system (latency). If these needs are not met in an organization, the level of group cohesiveness would not be high enough to keep the group functioning effectively. Sufficient levels of integration and latency cannot be established in an organization, without some level of mutual trust. Based on the postulation that there seems to be a link between principal behaviors and levels of faculty trust, an effort will be made in this study to isolate and measure those specific principal behaviors and their effect on faculty trust.

On a macro level, this link between principal behavior and faculty trust should be seen in the context of what practices make schools more effective. The context is framed around Ouchi's (1981) notion that trust helps create a positive school climate, Larson and LaFasto's (1989) finding that a positive school climate helps create an atmosphere in which team work can take place, and Little's (1982) additional findings that teamwork and collegial relations at a school site increase school effectiveness. There appears to be a thread running through the elements of trust, school climate, and school effectiveness. The missing link in this research base seems to be the apparent connection between the principal's behavior and how it effects levels of faculty trust. The purpose of this study is to illustrate the vital link between the principal's behavior and faculty trust, within the context of a school as an organization.

<u>Significance</u>

The major significance of this dissertation should be twofold. First, it will add to the scholarly body of knowledge regarding principal behaviors and how they may effect the climate of a school and, consequently, school effectiveness. It is a study that could be easily replicated and done on a much larger scale. If the results of further studies were consistent with these findings, there would then be an even more significant database regarding effective principal behaviors and practices.

This then would become the second and perhaps more valuable use of this study. The information gained from this research could have a direct impact on planning principal leadership training programs. If certain behaviors are consistently found to have a positive impact on faculty trust, then perhaps they can be learned by individuals and incorporated into their repertoire of leadership behaviors. If training programs can be developed from this data base, or if principals begin to practice these effective behaviors more routinely, then this exercise in academic research will have been more than justified.

Organization and Overview

This introductory chapter outlines some of the basic tenets of the literature on principal leadership behavior, trust, and school climate. Chapters Two through Five are organized in the conventionally described manner. Chapter Two reports background considerations of the problem and a review of recent literature focusing in on organizations, specific leadership behaviors, school climate, and faculty trust. An elaboration of the conceptual design of thesis and the application of the literature to the research question are also provided.

Chapter Three focuses on the research design and methodology of this study. This investigation was conducted in the following manner. Two questionnaires were administered to faculty members at 18 school sites in the State of California. They attempt to measure a principal's behavior, as well as levels of faculty trust. The results were tabulated and analyzed through a statistical model. Pearson correlations, t-tests, mean scores, and standard deviations are presented and analyzed.

Chapter Four includes a presentation and discussion of the research findings, and an analysis of the data and the three major hypotheses. Chapter Five relates to the conclusions, limitations, and areas for future research. The Appendix consists of raw data in the form of statistical printouts, letters, memorandum, questionnaires, list of sample schools, and test scores. Although the scope of this research is narrow and the generalizability limited, it is hoped that the cooperation of these 18 principals and their respective staffs will shed some light on the nature of their unique relationship in the school setting.

CHAPTER TWO

REVIEW OF LITERATURE

Overview

This chapter will review the role of a principal within the larger context of a school being an example of only one of many types of organizations. Major examples of organizations, as well as leadership in those organizations, will be reviewed in order to ground the school on a continuum of organizations—some large and some small, some formal and some informal, some public and some private. There will then be a brief discussion on the dynamics of the organization in the socialization process of those individuals who are members of the organization. The analysis of these dynamics will be based on the social theories and conceptual framework of Talcott Parsons.

From this point, the discussion will shift to a description of the school as an effective organization. An examination is then made regarding the culture and climate of the school and its relationship to school effectiveness. The analysis of school climate will be further refined and will delineate the concept of trust within the organization and how trust is related to a positive school climate. Next, a discussion on principal leadership behavior will lay the groundwork for the four principal behavioral constructs. Lastly, the thesis will narrow to the crucible: Can a principal's behavior impact the levels of faculty trust at a school site, and consequently improve the school climate?

Organization Types

A starting point in any leadership theory should begin with the work of Max Weber. Weber (1930) identifies three type of authority or leadership in organizations:

1. Traditional: legitimated by the sanctity of tradition. Usually defined by heredity, thought to be ordained by supernatural powers. Examples are monarchies, patriarchal/matriarchal families, small shop under a paternalistic/maternalistic boss.

2. Charismatic: legitimated by the dynamics of a social movement that challenges the status quo. Examples are revolutionary leaders, religious leaders, cult leaders.

3. Legal: legitimated by a belief in the supremacy of law and established social order. Examples are businesses, industry, military, government, schools.

The majority of organizations in the public sector are based on the "legal authority" model, although elements of the other typologies are found in public sector organizations. While some schools have some very influential informal leaders among the ranks of their faculty, they are not the leaders with the full legal authority vested by the State of California. This is an important distinction. The principal may be deemed with the legal authority to lead; however, they may not always be followed. For the purposes of this study, however, we will focus on the formal leader, the principal, who has the full legal authority, as well as legal responsibility to manage their schools.

Although Weber offers us a general definition of leadership and authority in an organization, the concept of organizations is one that requires further refinement. Blau and Scott (1962) have classified four distinct types of organizations, based on who the prime beneficiaries of that organization are. While Weber's constructs focus on the types of leadership within the organization, Blau and Scott focus on the functions of the organization. By briefly reviewing both constructs of leadership and function, a more thorough understanding of the leaders' behavior within those organizations can be gained. They are as follows:

1. <u>Mutual benefit associations</u>: prime benefit is the membership itself. Examples are political parties, trade unions, clubs, professional associations, religious sects, etc.

2. <u>Business concerns</u>: prime benefit is for the owners. Examples are industrial firms, mail-order houses, retail and wholesale concerns, banks, insurance companies, etc.

3. <u>Service organizations</u>: prime benefit is for the client. Examples are hospitals, social-work agencies, schools, etc.

4. <u>Commonweal organizations</u>: prime benefit is for the public at large. Examples are the military, police and fire service, State Department, etc.

Although Blau and Scott (1962) characterize the school as a "service" organization, the boundaries are certainly blurred between that category and the one described as "commonweal." What is clear, however, is that the school does function quite differently from the "business" and "mutual benefit" organizations. In this context we can take a closer look of what internal factors are found in the school, which we will characterize as a service organization.

<u>Organizational Context of Principal Leadership Behavior</u>

Educational leaders have been asked to perform in a societal context that seems to be demanding a complete systemic change. Glasman and Nevo (1988) note this theoretical connection between leadership and change very succinctly: "Whenever the society seeks fundamental changes it calls for improving leadership. It so happens that when the society seeks fundamental changes, it looks for changes in education and in schools and, therefore also, for improving educational leadership" (p. 14).

In order to understand the behaviors of a leader in an organization, it is first necessary to understand the dynamics of the organization. The leader of an organization operates in the context of the organization; therefore, a discussion on organizational theory is necessary before we can make sense of the behavior of the individuals within the organization. The connection between the leader and the organization is a difficult one to make; however, anyone who has ever been part of organization can attest to the fact that leaders do emerge, and indeed effect the functioning of the organization. Bennis and Nanus (1985), following interviews with 90 successful leaders, noted that leaders could actually "transform" organizations through creating a vision, developing enthusiasm by promoting shared meanings and symbols, establishing trust through modeling ideals, and the deployment of self through high self-esteem. Burns (1978) supported the notion that a leader can make a difference in an organization and describes the difference between a "transactional" versus "transformational" leader. The transactional leader merely manages the status quo interactions, whereas the transformational leader creates an environment where there is "the achievement of significant change that represents the collective interest of leaders and followers" (p. 251).

Implied in this concept of leadership is the notion that one also has the authority to lead. It can be argued, however, that authority and leadership are not the same. There are those individuals who wield official authority, but are not seen as leaders and, in fact, may be disdained by their followers. This may be exemplified in the military, where the drill instructor in boot camp has the full legal authority to order his/her charges to do the most extraordinary things, but who may also be disdained by the troops and who may not be seen as the leader who they would follow into battle.

Conversely, we are aware of those who have no official authority, but yet are looked upon as leaders. Following this same example in a combat setting, the person who ends up leading the troops in the field may not always be the designated officer; it could be a lowly buck private who raises to the level of hero by leading the entire platoon to safety. The point is that the leadership of an organization is not easily defined. This difference should always be kept in mind when discussing leadership behavior within an organization. The ideal, of course, is to have a leader who has the official power, as well as the loyalty and trust of their followers.

Role of the Organization

Parsons (1961) noted that all organizations must solve four basic problems if they are to survive:

1. Adaptation: the process of acquiring sufficient resources and accommodating to the environment.

2. Goal attainment: not only the attainment of the goal, but the process of setting goals that are considered to be vital to the life of the organization.

3. Integration: the process of maintaining the internal solidarity of the system.

4. Latency: the preserving of the distinctive value system unique to the organization.

Etzioni (1975) has taken these four functions and reduced them into two basic needs for an organization: (a) the instrumental needs of input and allocation, and (b) the expressive needs of social and normative integration. Parsons (1967) also noted that schools, like most organizations, have three basic functions: (a) the technical, which is concerned with the teaching and learning process; (b) the managerial, which controls the internal administration of the organization; and (c) the institution, which links the school with the community.

This Parsonian model provides the framework for the study of the school as an effective organization. It also provides the context for the study of the behaviors of principals and how they affect the organization. It is of interest to note that much of the current effective schools research seems to rely on the technical and managerial aspects found in this Parsonian model, and seemingly ignores the institutional aspects of linking the school to the community.

The recent effective schools research, Edmonds (1979) and Rosenholtz (1985), focuses on the Parsonian technical concepts of the teaching and learning process and their relationship to adaptation and goal attainment as well as the managerial attempt to control the internal administration of the organization (i.e., integration and latency). The problems of integration and latency are the organization's attempt to establish internal cohesion and identity or, in other words, the organization's attempt to establish a unique identity or culture.

Parsonian Framework

The conceptual framework of this study is based on a sociological rather than a psychological model. The intention of this study was to investigate group interactions with a leader in the context of an organization. The focus was on the perceptions within the group rather than psychological profiles of the individual leaders; therefore, the sociological perspective was selected. The sociological theory that best describes this behavior within an organization is offered by Parsons (1961). The Parsonian model notes that organizations are guided by a strong need to solve particular problems in order to serve the needs of it members and clients, and ultimately survive. The organization must fulfill the needs found in the functions of (a) adaptation, (b) goal attainment, (c) integration, and (d) latency. Parsons (1967) also noted that schools had three distinct levels of control over these activities: (a) the technical (teaching process), (b) the managerial (principal/faculty interactions), and (c) the institutional (legitimacy in the community). Hoy et al. (1991) supports this notion by noting that a healthy school is one in which the technical, managerial, and institutional are in harmony.

The focus of this study centers on the functions of integration and latency. This is not to say that the other functions are not of value to scrutinize; on the contrary, one may argue that a group could not exist without them. The functions of integration and latency are, however, strongly related to the concept of trust and therefore are core concepts in this study.

The need for integration in an organization is the need for a group to have some sense about what it does on a daily basis. It is a need for expectations to be set, and rules to be followed. Each organization must have some reasonable norms that have been set through the mutual interactions of the leader and the group member. If these norms are not developed in the group, there would be such confusion and tension that the group would have great difficulty trying to exist.

The latency needs of preserving a distinctive value system in the organization can also be viewed as the culture of the organization. Culture is unique in each organization and is a result of the interrelationships developed between the faculty and the principals. It is based on the unique mutual interactions between those two groups. It is the blending of the latency (group culture) needs and needs for integration (teacher affiliation) that give each group its identity. This does not in any way minimize the importance and impacts of adaptation (securing of resources) and goal attainment (achievement of group objectives) on the character and definition of the organization. They are not, however, the primary aspects of organizational theory that are the focus of this study.

In the case of a school, this translates into the principal's behavior being consistent with what they said they would do. Henderson and Hoy (1982) define this as "leader authenticity." The authentic leader is seen as accountable, non-manipulative, and salient of themselves over their role. There is a match between the principal's beliefs and philosophies, and those of the faculty. If there is not a match, the chance for being effective is lessened. This concept of principal authenticity is strongly related to the integration and latency needs of the school organization. In fact, Blumberg and Greenfield (1980) found that principal authenticity and trust are related. Likewise, Ouchi (1981) maintained that to foster this environment of trust, the leader must demonstrate openness, honesty, and candor. This authenticity of behavior by the principal and the attention to both the latency and integration needs of the organization are found to be common factors in effective schools research.

Characteristics of Effective Schools

Schools, like most other organizations, can be characterized as a having a set of goals that the majority of members of that organization are striving to achieve. Edmonds' (1979) work on effective schools is comprehensive, and identifies the following characteristics of effective schools. It should be noted that this particular effective schools research is based on data obtained from urban school districts. This delimits its use; however, it is still recognized as a benchmark piece in effective schools research. The characteristics include:

1. A pervasive and broadly understood academic focus or school mission.

2. Careful monitoring of school achievement as a basis for program evaluation.

3. Teachers who believe in and exhibit high expectations that all students can master the curriculum.

4. A safe and orderly school climate conducive to learning.

5. A principal who is an instructional leader.

A common thread found through the research on effective schools was that of a strong emphasis on the managerial function. In effective schools, there seems to be a strong leadership component. The leadership does not always derive from the formal structure (i.e., the principal). There are some schools where the leadership is derived from informal structures (i.e., teachers, vice principals, or other mid-level school site positions) (Slater, 1991).

Heck et al. (1990) described several behaviors, including communicating instructional goals, working to keep faculty morale high, and establishing an orderly environment to enhance school climate as factors in having an effect on student outcomes. These and other principal behaviors, such as securing resources for the program, promoting curricular programs, and evaluating curricular programs, were found to positively effect student achievement.

In the effective schools research, there was a strong agreement that common goals were necessary for a schools to be successful. Rosenholtz (1985) found that these organizational goals were incentives that attracted teachers to successful schools. The teachers in the effective school identified their personal goals with that of the organization. These common goals would then combine into collaborative norms over a period of time. These normative behaviors resulted in teachers who interacted to a greater extent on the basis of professional concerns, rather than social matters. These professional interactions took place with a greater frequency and with a larger number of colleagues. A key factor here is that these professional interactions took place not only with teachers, but also included the principal.

Achieving consensus was also found to be characteristic of the effective school. It could be more readily achieved when teachers were involved and willing to participate in technical decisions pertaining to their particular school site. Wynne (1980) found that this included areas of instruction and materials, as well as school-wide goals. In general, teachers seemed to teach better when they worked together. Little (1982) found that when teachers were isolated, their mode of interaction seemed to be sympathy or complaint; however, when they worked in a collegial model, their interactions focused on the healthy exchange of ideas. This, in turn, gave rise to greater experimentation and increased effectiveness, which reinforced the task-oriented level of collegial instruction.

Wynne (1980) also found that participation in decision making was a factor in effective schools. This was especially true in the area of technical decision making (i.e., selecting instructional materials, determining appropriate instructional methods and techniques, and establishing general instructional policies). This teacher willingness to participate in technical decision making included the adoption of school-wide goals. Azumi and Madhere (1983) noted that teachers who had less input in the setting of instructional goals had greater uncertainty about their capacity to bring about improvement of student performance. This was supported by Bishop's (1977) work on new teachers functioning in isolated settings. New teachers who were isolated developed a custodial student control ideology, while those in collegial settings maintained a more humanistic work orientation toward the individual student, and were consequently more effective.

The literature on effective schools indicates a connection between school effectiveness and organizational health. The concept of organizational health seems to be better described as a school culture or climate.

Culture and Climate in the School Setting

Within the organization there are a series of human interactions that take place. These cumulative interactions result in a collection of individuals who at some point begin to act as what is considered to be a group. Barnard (1938) and Mayo (1945) noted that significant norms, sentiments, values, and interactions emerge in the workplace. They described the nature and the function of the organization and, in so doing, described some of the factors that make group dynamics so complex. Selznick (1957) further stated that organizations were institutions that are "infused with value beyond the technical requirements at hand" (p. 17). This infusion of value then produced a distinct identity of the organization that went beyond the formal descriptions and official flow charts. This value infusion is what is commonly referred to as a group identity, or more recently referred to as group culture or climate.

Miles (1969) described this concept of value or group identity in the organization as "organizational health." This notion of organizational health maintains that organizations are able to survive because they are making continuous adjustments to adapt to the outside environment. This implies that although the core values may be maintained, there must be some adjustments made in order for the organization to maintain its effectiveness. A member of an organization is influenced in many ways. The socialization process is a factor that must be considered when examining leadership in an organization.

Halpin (1966) was one of the first to conceptualize what we call organizational climate. From the data, Halpin derived a model that described an open healthy climate that was indicative of an effective school. This model described a school that had centered leadership by the principal, a committed faculty, little burdensome paperwork, simple rules, and a low-profile level of supervision. Hoy et al. (1991) described these healthy schools as places that promoted good mental health because of cooperative and supportive relations. These healthy schools had low levels of frustration and high levels of morale, with real engagement with the task at hand. The converse was found to be true in the closed climate. In a closed climate, both teachers and administrators were disengaged; individuals just went through the motions. The principal emphasized unnecessary rules and asked for burdensome records. Morale was low and frustration was high in the closed-climate school. There was also a basic lack of trust in the principals' ability to lead. Porter, Steers, Mowday, and Boulian (1974) found that healthy effective schools had committed teachers who were found to have accepted the goals of the organization. It was found that these teachers were willing to put forth extra effort, and had a desire to remain as productive members in the current school assignment.

The climate or culture of a school is not easily explained or quantified. The terms "culture" and "climate" have been used interchangeably; however, technically this is incorrect. Hoy et al. (1991) described anthropology and sociology as disciplines that focus on culture, whereas social psychology and psychology would focus on climate. Ashforth (1985) referred to the term "culture" as consisting of shared assumptions, values, and norms about the way people act in groups. Climate, on the other hand, was defined by the shared perceptions of members of a particular organization about the feelings within the organization.

Perhaps another way of looking at this would be to say that a school culture is what range of behaviors have developed in the group, whereas the climate would be what the members actually say about the feelings in the group within the culture. The term "culture" may be misleading because it is usually seen as explaining deeply imbedded concepts found in larger segments of the population. Hoy and Miskel (1987) defined climate as the relatively enduring quality of a school environment that is experienced by participants, affects their behavior, and is based on their collective perception of behavior in schools.

Little (1982) also found that in successful schools, teachers valued and participated in norms of collegiality and strived toward continuous improvement through experimentation. They pursued a greater range of professional interaction with their colleagues, including administrators. One of the key elements in a healthy school climate was the level of teacher participation in the decision making. It was also noted that in all schools that staff characterized as highly collegial, teachers viewed the principal as an active endorser and participant in collegial work.

As was noted earlier, the healthy and effective school must satisfy the Parsonian model that goals be achieved and that group members be integrated into the organization. In order for this to occur, there must be an atmosphere or climate where these initiations can take place. The literature indicated that faculty trust was an important intervening variable between principal leadership behavior and organizational effectiveness.

Trust

Hoy and Kupersmith (1985) have attempted to scrutinize and observe this concept of trust, and have developed an instrument to measure it. They define trust as a "general expectancy held by a work group that the word, action, and written or oral statement of another individual, group, or organization can be relied upon" (p. 108). Hoy et al. (1991) state that trust impacts both the instrumental and expressive activities of the organization. Their research also indicated a significant correlation between organizational health and the feelings of trust toward colleagues as well as trust toward the principal. They found the principal's behavior was instrumental in developing an atmosphere of trust. Principals who were persuasive, worked effectively with their superiors, and who demonstrated an independence in thought and action promoted mutual trust among faculty.

Larson and LaFasto (1989) identified four factors that were necessary for a climate of trust to exist in an organization: (a) honesty—integrity, no lies or exaggerations; (b) openness—a willingness to share, and a receptivity to information, perceptions, ideas; (c) consistency—predictable behavior and responses; and (d) respect—treating people with dignity and fairness.

Golembiewski and McConkie (1975) noted that trust was an important aspect of life that effects individual and group behavior in all social systems and is strongly linked to general confidence and overall optimism in the organization. Ouchi (1981) went as far to say that trust is the fundamental feature of superior and subordinate relationships that pervades most successful management practices. Hughes (1974) argued that trust is necessary for establishing effective interpersonal relations, and Gibb (1969) notes the connection with establishing leadership patterns. Although there is an element of concern and fear for not following the orders or directives of superiors in organizations, behaviors based on mutual respect and trust are more beneficial to the organization. Trust is perhaps one of the most important factors connecting a member of an organization to the group, as well as the leader. Schools are an example of an organization where trust is also necessary for the goals of the group to be achieved effectively. The connection between effective leadership and trust in is apparent. What needs closer scrutiny is whether or not there is a particular leadership style or behavior that engenders higher levels of trust.

Faculty Trust

The research indicates that trust is a basic characteristic of effective organizational cultures. Hoy et al. (1991) note that healthy school climates were characterized by many of the same attributes stressed in effective schools' literature. They noted that consideration and institutional integrity were the best predictors of teachers having trust in the principal. Institutional integrity here is defined as the process whereby a principal protects and buffers the teacher from unwarranted outside influences such as parental complaints, classroom interruptions, and tedious record-keeping requirements. This so-called buffering of teachers from negative outside influences is one of the most powerful factors in the building of faculty trust in the principal.

There is an important connection between this involvement process and the building of trust; that is the concept of communication. Sullivan (1988) identified communicating candidly, confronting issues, and using each other's resourcefulness as factors that affect climate and increase the likelihood of teams attaining their missions, goals, and objectives. Larson and LaFasto (1989) support this finding by noting that the effectiveness of a team is improved by having higher levels of trust, which allowed them to be self-correcting and free to question previous decisions. This attempt to unite a faculty through collaboration is frequently reflected in the language used to accomplish this goal. Blase and Kirby (1992) found such words as "family," "team," "cooperation," "community," and "harmony" were used over and over again. This "inclusion strategy" was found to increase faculty morale and trust.

Glickman (1990) found evidence of improved achievement as well as improved school climate in schools where teachers had a voice in school governance. An interesting side note of this study is the irony to be found in teacher empowerment. It seemed that the more successful the school and level of teacher empowerment, the less successful it was for others to emulate. This was ascribed to the fact that for schools to be successful they truly had to find their own way. Using a model already developed by another group negated the first step for successful teacher empowerment, which was simply the agreement to make decisions for themselves.

Parsons (1961) viewed trust as an intrinsic element of pattern maintenance in an organization. Healthy and effective schools fulfill the requirement that goals be achieved and that members are integrated into the organization. Hughes (1974) also noted that trust was necessary for establishing effective interpersonal relations in organizations. Paul (1982) reinforced this notion with his findings that trust was a necessary factor for building teamwork.

Tarter, Bliss, and Hoy (1989) defined faculty trust "as the teachers confidence that the principal will keep his or her word and will act in the teachers best interest" (p. 295). They found that the leadership behavior of the principal, rather than the interrelationships among teachers, predicted the level of trust in the organization. Principals who were helpful and genuinely concerned about professional and personal welfare of their teachers and who were open, friendly, and collegial were most likely to have the trust of their teachers. Nearly 20% of the variance in faculty trust in the principal was attributed to the principal's supportiveness. This personal relationship of simply showing teachers that they were respected was also a powerful factor in building levels of trust.

Gomez (1987), in a study of elementary school principals and teachers, found that teachers identified being trusted by the principal as one of the most influential principal behaviors. Johnston and Venable (1986) found that elementary teachers tended to respond more to a personal relationship of consideration with the principal rather than the joint involvement in decision making.

Deal (1987) has noted that school effectiveness literature ignores the impacts of significant interpersonal skills, and argues that schools should be examined under multiple lenses such as school climate, parental satisfaction, and student absenteeism, and similar factors in order to determine effectiveness. It should not solely rely on student achievement test data. Greenfield (1982) found that effective principals had high needs for expressing and receiving warmth and affection, thus increasing the likelihood of trust. Weiss (1990), however, noted that this involvement must be viewed as authentic and as consistent with the belief system of the principal. If the level of involvement was mundane and cursory, it would raise the levels of resentment rather than trust.

Blase and Kirby (1992) found that the most effective and most frequently reported behavior of principals to effect teacher loyalty and trust was the use of praise. Greenfield (1987) noted that the significance of praise in effecting behavior of employees may seem obvious, but it is an area that has been largely unattended in the literature on effective schools. It was also noted that the use of praise, to be effective, must be viewed as being sincere, genuine, and as a natural part of the principal's character. Henderson and Hoy (1982) found that principals who treated teachers with respect, acted on their own values and beliefs rather than in compliance with bureaucratic roles, and held themselves accountable for their school's success were considered to be "authentic." They were considered to be authentic because their behavior seemed to be consistent with their beliefs. Since they were willing to practice what they preached, they engendered higher levels of faculty satisfaction and trust.

Russell et al. (1985) found that a principal's willingness to "back up" teachers in their decisions regarding student misbehavior to be a powerful form of influence over teacher behaviors and attitudes. Blase and Kirby (1992) also found that principal support increased teacher confidence which, in turn, increased their effectiveness in the classroom. This support was also manifested in principals' listening skills, giving of advice, and problem-solving skills. When conflicts arose with parents, these effective principals publicly supported their teachers. They influenced faculty morale because they were honest, caring, and non-manipulative. Heck et al. (1990) also found that protection of instructional time created a positive attitude and feelings of trust in teachers. This included protecting teachers from unwarranted interruptions by parents, students, and teachers, as well as administrators.

Kouzes and Posner (1990) studied the personal traits and characteristics most admired in leaders and found the overwhelming choice and test of one's ability was honesty. Foster (1991) noted that administrators could help transform schooling through open critique, caring, and inclusion. It was noted that this style of leadership was based on values of trust honesty, optimism, and consideration for people's personal needs. Foster went on to say that effective principals were successful because of their "personal and moral presence, their sense of 'what's right', and their attention to people's needs" (p. 7). This encapsulated in the now famous Bennis (1985) quote, "Managers are people who do things right and leaders are people who do the right thing" (p. 21). The literature supports the basic postulate that trust is related to a healthy school climate.

Principal Leadership Behavior

Principals, like all leaders, rely on a specific style of leadership to accomplish their goals. It is usually a combination of personality and organizational structure, as well as the situation, that determines the behavior. There are some models, however, that would be helpful to illustrate. Moser (1957) identified three styles of administrative behavior. Each style of leadership had different effects on teachers.

1. Nomothetic: Characterized by behavior that stresses goal accomplishment, rules and regulations, and centralized authority at the expense of the individual.

2. Idiographic: Characterized by behavior that stresses the individuality of people, minimum rules and regulations, decentralized authority, and highly individualized relationships with subordinates.

3. Transactional: Characterized by a balance of nomothetic and idiographic behavior, and a judicious use of each style as the occasion demands.

The transactional leader was found to be most effective, especially when there was congruence between what behavior the teacher expected from the principal and the actual behavior.

Campbell (1957) found that when the principal's role expectations were in agreement with the teachers' wants and needs, the following results were observed: (a) the teachers expressed a higher level of job satisfaction, (b) the principals rated the teachers as more effective, and (c) teachers expressed a higher level of confidence in the principal's leadership. Isherwood (1973) found that principals who demonstrated charisma, expertise, and human relations skills heightened teachers' loyalty to the principal and improved teacher satisfaction. Treslan and Ryan (1986) also found that teachers were much more responsive to a principal's influence attempts based on human relation skills and technical expertise rather than use of hierarchical authority.

The notion of leadership, being that of a strictly hierarchical structure within a tightly ruled organization, does not fit the model of the effectively run school. Foskett (1967) was one of the first to identify the highly ambiguous nature of the principalship and the conflicting demands surrounding the role in the school organization. Weick (1976) describes this adaptation of the organization as "loosely coupled systems." He notes that "coupling," defined as "give an order or set a policy, and have it followed without question," is no longer an effective model. Instead, the "looseness," defined as experimentation, confusion, persistence, risk taking, and randomness, are what seems to define leadership in effective organizations. Perhaps the most classic study to date, which fits this notion of role ambiguity, was done on the everyday life of the an elementary principal. Wolcott's (1973) ethnography demonstrated the inadequate time resources as well as the conflicting demands of the elementary principal, made for a job that defied description based on the standard models of organizational management.

These findings do not support the effectiveness of the standard top-down management structure that is found in most nomothetic organizations. Peterson (1978) reinforced this notion by describing the role of the principal as one that involved interactions that were many, highly varied, fragmented, and very brief in time. Sproul (1981) concluded that these severe restraints on principals' time could, however, serve a useful function:

Given a weak technology and a particular configuration of loose connections, these attention patterns are quite understandable. The manager who can keep people happy, supplied with resources, and not inquire too closely into their activities is doing a good job. In an ambiguous world, comfort and solidarity are derived from social pleasantries. (p. 121)

Bossert et al. (1982) found that there was a link between leadership behavior and teacher performance. Principal behaviors such as goal setting, evaluating, monitoring, and modeling effected a school setting on two levels. One was the organizational, which included such factors as curriculum, pedagogy, and scheduling. The other was climate, which included such factors as commitment, morale, and trust.

Heck et al. (1990) described examples of climate factors, such as communicating instructional goals, working on faculty morale, and establishing an orderly environment that enhanced school morale. Other identified leadership behaviors that were more directly related to organization included developing school-wide goals, securing resources, and evaluating programs. They concluded that if both of these organizational factors were found in principal decision making that there would be an increase in student achievement. In summary they stated:

Our results indicate that many of the important instructional leadership variables influencing school achievement are not related to regular clinical supervision of teachers. Many behaviors which are more informal and strategic cluster into the constructs of instructional organization and school climate and impact student achievement as well. Some of these efforts involve clarifying, coordinating, and communicating a unified school educational purpose to teachers students and the community. Effective principals appear to build a sense of teamwork at the school. (pp. 120-121)

Rosenholtz (1985) found that principals of effective schools had a unitary mission of improved student learning. These principals organizationally buffered teachers against unreasonable demands from the community so that their efforts could be directed to teaching and raising student achievement. They also fostered opportunities to achieve these student academic goals in cooperation with ones teaching colleagues.

Hoy et al. (1990) found that the value of highly assertive leadership that Edmonds (1979) and others claimed to be so instrumental in effective school was not supported in their sample study. Bossert et al. (1982) further stated that the principal's major role was that of affecting climate and the instructional organization, and in so doing indirectly impact the achievement of students. The implication here is that by building trust and a positive climate, a principal can indirectly improve the academic performance of students in their school. This is a powerful concept that is in need of further study and refinement. Hoy et al. (1990) attempted to make this point clearly and emphasized the importance of climate:

> It may be that some principals can directly affect student learning by manipulating the instructional organization. Our findings, however, support the notion that the principal's influence is indirect, provided his/her actions lead to the development of a climate with a strong academic emphasis.
>
> ....Our data support this hypothesis even controlling for SES. (p. 275)

Hoy, Tarter, and Forsyth (1978) found that the principal's balanced use of formal and informal authority was most effective in creating a positive school climate. Two of the major components that were found to build collaboration, trust, and loyalty were the following:

1. Consideration: defined as the ability for the principal to project a real concern for the well-being of staff members.

2. Non-authoritarian behavior: defined as the ability of the principal to lead through a philosophy of mutual respect and trust.

It is apparent that one of the keys to principal effectiveness is the positive use of influence on teachers. Muth (1973) noted that principals' use of persuasion was significantly related to the degree of consensus among teachers.

Johnson (1984) noted that principal expertise, personal example, distribution of resources, and expressed interest impacted favorably on students. Johnston and Venable (1986) linked effective participatory decision making to greater teacher loyalty to principals. Reitzug (1989), in another study of elementary principals, noted that consistency of behavior and a high level of interactions were characteristics of principals in effective schools. The principals in instructionally effective schools had 52% more instructional leadership interactions and spent twice as much time in such interactions. Even the simple behavior of a daily greeting of teachers by the principal was noted as being a positive influence in creating trust in the effective schools.

Larson and LaFasto (1989) identified several sets of leadership variables that were found in high-performance organizations. One of the most important was the creation of a supportive decision-making climate. They noted that the effective leader created a climate that unleashed people's bias toward action, which in turn created enthusiasm and commitment to the team objective. The review of the literature is clear; principals do affect the performance of their schools. If we can identify behaviors that will create this environment for transformation of a school, we will have made significant contribution to the literature on leadership and effective schools.

Summary of Principal Behaviors Effecting Faculty Trust

The review of the literature indicated that there were specific behaviors practiced by principals that may indeed have impact on attitudes of trust among teachers. A number of authentic behaviors were found consistently in leaders that lead effective organizations. The focus of this study is to determine if these principal behaviors can be measured and subsequently correlated with levels of faculty trust. The importance of linking such behaviors with levels of faculty trust is the additional relationship found between levels of trust and a positive school climate.

These identified principal behaviors fall into four specific categories. They have been constructed from behavioral characteristics found in the review of the literature. They include what is defined as Praising, Buffering, Involving, and Caring behaviors. These are certainly not the only behaviors that may effect faculty trust, and some have undoubtedly more impact than others, but they are the core principal behaviors that are analyzed in this study. They include the following:

1. Praising behaviors: These principal behaviors include recognizing a faculty member for their contributions to the organization. In order for the principal to be effective, the praise should be specific and authentic. It must also focus on the work or task, not the person. The praise may take the form of individual and/or group praise, and it may be both verbal and written. Effective principals also use nonverbal gestures such as smiles, nods, and touches to communicate approval. Written praise can range from formal letters of recognition or awards assemblies, to informal notes left on the teacher's desk. This praising behavior is usually characterized as being both simple and brief.

2. Buffering behaviors: These principal behaviors protect the teacher's time from any undue loss of instructional minutes. This includes minimizing parent, student, and administrative interruptions. Effective principals also publicly support the teacher when their behaviors and practices come under criticism or question. This includes the principal's backing teachers in dealing with discipline problems. Buffering also takes the form of

limiting the number of staff meetings, as well as the amount of routine paperwork. The principal's backing of teachers is a show of respect for the difficulty and pressures that teachers deal with on a daily basis. This respect is then returned in the increased levels of faculty trust.

3. Involving behaviors: These principal behaviors focus on the effort to involve others in decision making. This is most effective when the outcomes will have a direct effect on the day-to-day activities of those making the decision. Effective principals create a climate for participation by delegating responsibility to willing teachers who have the relevant knowledge and expertise. They are willing to accept the decision of the group even though they may not fully agree. They are also aware of the fact that teachers are professionals who do not want to be involved in trivial time-consuming matters. When teachers feel that their time is wasted and that the decision making is not having a direct impact on them, they build up resentments that undermine the program. The manifestation of this principal behavior is the formation of site-based leadership teams that increase routine interaction with teachers, parents, and students. These interactions must result in decisions that reflect the concerns of the faculty in order for the involving behaviors to be effective.

4. Caring behaviors: These principal behaviors focus on the genuine concern for the welfare of the teacher. Effective principals demonstrate concern for the physical and emotional health of their teachers. This is seen as celebrating the positive events in teachers' lives, while offering support for the hardships. They listen closely and offer advice for problems that are both personal and professional. Special consideration is shown when mistakes are made so that teachers will not become discouraged and afraid to try new things. The caring behavior is seen as being honest and nonmanipulative. There is a sincere interest in the personal lives of teachers, without being overly intrusive.

By looking at this wide spectrum of principal behaviors we can gain valuable insights into the key elements that impact schools. This study focuses on principal behaviors and how they impact the affective domain in the workplace. It is my observation that this aspect of leadership needs much closer scrutiny.

Much of the current research focuses on the organizational and technical aspects of the organization. For the practitioner, this study will be helpful in establishing a guide or model for an effective principal. For the researcher, a baseline will be established that should encourage further study.

Assumptions for Research Questions

The framework for this research is based on a central assumption found throughout the review of the literature: There exists a set of behavioral characteristics among principals that seems to have an effect on levels of faculty trust. This relates back to the Parsonian model that describes the need for the organization to have internal solidarity (integration), as well as a distinctive value system (latency). If these needs are not met by the organization, the level of group cohesiveness would not be high enough to keep the group functioning effectively. In order for this study to progress, several assumptions must be made.

After a careful review of the literature, the following postulates about faculty trust and principal behaviors can be deduced:

1. There must be some significant level of trust in a school between the principal and faculty in order for the school to function effectively.

2. There are specific and observable principal behaviors that can be identified and described as having positive impacts on faculty trust.

3. The concept of trust can be defined and measured in some objective and quantifiable manner.

4. A correlation can be made between these specific and observable behaviors principal behaviors and levels of faculty trust.

5. Schools that are considered to be effective have higher levels of faculty trust than schools that are considered to be less effective.

<u>Research Questions</u>

There are four basic questions that will be answered:

1. Do specific and identifiable principal behaviors have a positive effect on levels of faculty trust?

2. If so, what are these specific and identifiable principal behaviors effecting levels of faculty trust?

3. If there is an effect on levels of faculty trust, which of these specific and identifiable behaviors have the most powerful impacts?

4. Do schools that are considered to be effective have higher levels of faculty trust in the principal than those schools that are considered not to be effective?

This set of assumptions and research questions has been carefully drawn from the most current literature on educational leadership. It stimulates the investigation between school effectiveness and a principal's leadership behaviors. Hypotheses addressing these questions and assumptions are stated in the following chapter.

CHAPTER THREE
METHODOLOGY

Introduction

The purpose of this dissertation is to investigate the association between behaviors of elementary school principals and levels of faculty trust. In addition, an attempt was made to analyze the possible differences in principal behaviors in schools that performed at different levels—more specifically, a comparison of schools that achieved higher-level scores on a standardized test to those who scored at a lower level on the same test. The intention in the comparison of high- and low-achieving schools was to identify schools that had similar demographic characteristics so that intervening variables such as socioeconomic status (SES), number of Limited English Proficient (LEP) students, and student mobility would not skew the results of the comparison. By limiting the sample to similar-type schools, the focus was maintained on the principal behaviors and trust, and not on the demographic impacts.

The data for the study was collected through a questionnaire administered to teachers at the selected schools. The statistical tool used to analyze the relationship between the principal be-haviors and faculty trust was the Pearson's Product Moment Correlation Coefficient. An independent t-test was also used to compare the lower-performing schools with the higher-performing schools. A one-tailed t-test was used to compare groups and to indicate direction. Mean scores and standard deviations for all questions for the 18 schools were reported. An analysis of the questionnaires and data collection procedures are also included in this chapter.

Overview of Questionnaires

Two questionnaires were distributed to each of the school sites, one measuring levels of faculty trust and the other measuring the four principal behaviors. There was a 7-question Trust in Principal Scale constructed by Hoy and Kupersmith (1985) and a 20-question Principal Behavior Scale that was constructed by the author of this study. They both utilized a 6-point Likert scale, with a score of six being the most positive response and a score of one being the most negative. Embedded in the Principal Behavior Scale were 20 questions relating to the four principal behavioral constructs.

Questions 1, 5, 9, 13, and 17 related to Praising behaviors:
1. Teachers in this school receive letters and notes praising their action, from the principal.
5. Teachers in this school are recognized at award ceremonies.
9. Teachers in this school receive verbal praise and encouragement from the principal.
13. Teachers in this school receive nonverbal praise such as smiles, handshakes, and pats on the back, from the principal.
17. Teachers in this school feel that praise for their teaching is an important aspect related to their job satisfaction.

Questions 2, 6, 10, 14, and 18 related to Buffering behaviors:
2. Teachers in this school feel that the principal tries to protect their instructional time.
6. Teachers in this school feel that the principal defends them against unwarranted parent complaints.

10. Teachers in this school feel that the principal handles student discipline in a manner that reflects support of teachers.
14. Teachers in this school feel that their meetings are productive.
18. Teachers in this school feel that they are asked to do a fair amount of paperwork.

Questions 3, 7, 11, 15, and 19 related to <u>Involving</u> behaviors:
3. Teachers in this school are consulted on decisions that affect what happens in their classrooms.
7. Teachers and parents meet with the principal on a routine basis to assist in site level decision making.
11. When the principal asks for advice from teachers, it is taken seriously and acted upon.
15. Teachers in this school are given a wide range of responsibilities by the principal.
19. Teachers who are involved in making site level decisions with the principal feel that their time is being used productively, and that they do have an impact on the final decision.

Questions 4, 8, 12, 16, and 20 related to <u>Caring</u> behaviors:
4. Teachers in this school feel that the principal shows genuine concern about their personal lives.
8. Teachers in this school feel that the principal shows genuine concern about their professional growth.
12. Teachers in this school try new ideas and programs.
16. Teachers in this school feel that the principal shows a genuine interest in regarding their family members.
20. The principal really cares about the general well-being of the entire staff.

The <u>Trust in Principal Scale</u> questions were as follows:
1. The teachers in this school are suspicious of most of the principal's actions.
2. The teachers in this school have faith in the integrity of the principal.

3. The principal takes unfair advantage of the teachers in this school.
4. The principal in this school typically acts with the best interests of the teachers in mind.
5. Teachers in this school often question the motives of the principal.
6. Teachers in this school trust the principal.
7. The principal in this school keeps his/her word.

Data Sample

The schools that were identified for the final study were selected from a 100-school comparison band of California public elementary schools who participated in the 1992-93 California Learning Assessment System (CLAS) testing program. These 100 schools had almost identical levels of socioeconomic status (SES), student mobility, and the number of students who were Limited English Proficient (LEP). This 100-school band was generated from a database that was developed by the California State Department of Education and was based on information collected when the CLAS was administered. In general terms, these 100 schools would be characterized as successful upper-middle-class socioeconomic-level schools, with few of the major problems that seem to impact schools in some of our larger urban settings. The selection of this type of higher SES sample was purposeful due to the fact that a conscious effort was made not to compare schools that had major demographic differences. It would be more difficult to try to analyze such variables as Trust, Caring, Involving, Buffering, and Praising, where overwhelming demographic factors and potential school dysfunction are experienced.

As Kozol (1991) has noted, many lower SES schools are faced with such a multitude of problems that faculty and administration are just attempting to maintain a safe and orderly environment and survive each day. This dissatisfaction in our urban schools has recently been corroborated in a Harris (1995) survey conducted among urban and suburban teachers in the United States. The results indicated that urban teachers reported much less satisfaction in their jobs, feel less likely to be respected or recognized for good performance, and feel that problems have dramatically worsened in the past few years. The negative impacts of lower SES demographic factors on student performance and school effectiveness was supported by Coleman's (1966) conclusive findings that SES is still the dominant factor when evaluating school effectiveness, and significantly outweighed all other factors.

In an attempt to provide as much focus as possible, the sample was drawn from elementary schools rather than a combination of elementary and secondary schools. The elementary school structure, and its related school culture, is usually quite different than that of a secondary school. The size of most public high schools is much larger than the elementary schools, and there are vast differences in the needs of students as well as staff.

The type of student and administrative contacts experienced by teachers at these different levels made a comparison of elementary schools to secondary schools inappropriate for this study. In most cases, there is much more direct contact with an elementary-level principal and faculty than there is with a secondary principal and faculty. Many faculty contacts at the high school level are with assistant principals and counselors, so it would be difficult, at best, to attempt to isolate the effects of principal behaviors where there seem to be fewer direct contacts with the principal.

Hoy et al. (1991) have also noted this difference between elementary and secondary schools and went to the extent of developing four different instruments to measure school openness and organizational health specific to secondary and elementary levels. The Organizational Climate Description Questionnaires for Elementary and Secondary (OCDQ-RE, OCDQ-RS) measure school openness, and the Organizational Health (OHI-E, OHI) Inventory for Elementary and Secondary measure the school health.

> Secondary schools are more complex than elementary schools; they have greater specialization and division of labor and more rules and regulations. Typically they are larger, often serving as a receiving school for a number of elementary schools. It should come as no surprise to

learn that an instrument designed to measure the climate of one kind of school is not entirely satisfactory for another. (p. 46)

Demographic Variables

The sample schools were selected based on the achievement scores of fourth grade students on the spring 1993 California Learning Assessment System (CLAS test). The following comparison is made to highlight the differences with other schools in the State of California in these four demographic variables. This comparison shows that the schools selected for this study were at a higher SES level. The rankings and scores in the 100 school band for the four SES/demographic variables were as follows:

Socioeconomic index. The score in this area was a 3.97, whereas the state average was 3.06. This was an indicator of the occupations of parents of students. The occupations were rated as follows:

1. Unknown
2. Unskilled employee
3. Technical, Sales, Administrative Support
4. Skilled and semi-skilled employees
5. Managers and Professionals

The socioeconomic index was the average (mean) of these values of the students in this grade. The higher the value, the higher the socioeconomic level of the community served by this school. The mean scores of the schools in the sample were almost one full level above the state mean scores.

Aid to Families with Dependent Children (AFDC). The score in this area was 2.5%, whereas the state score was 20.4%. This was an indicator of the percent of students who were receiving government assistance. For each school, the number of students from families receiving AFDC in the school attendance area was divided by the sum of the public and private school enrollment in the area to yield the percent AFDC. The percent score in this area indicated a major difference in the number of students receiving government assistance. There were far fewer students living below the poverty level in the schools chosen for the study compared to other schools in the State of California.

Limited English Proficient (LEP). The score in this area was 13.9 %, whereas the state was 19.7 %. This was an indicator of the percent of students who were considered to be Limited English Proficient (LEP). Teachers were asked to classify each student's English language fluency. Those that were considered to be LEP students were considered to be Tested Limited English Proficient and Non-tested Limited English Proficient. A LEP student was not required to be assessed in 1993 if the student had been enrolled in the United States for less than 30 school months. In addition, schools were allowed to exempt a LEP student enrolled in the United States for over 30 school months if the student was currently receiving primary language instruction in a language other than English. Again, we see a significant difference between schools in the sample selection when compared to those in the state.

Student mobility. The score was 11.3%, whereas the state was 12.0%. Student mobility was measured by the percent of students newly enrolled in the school district during the last year. This was the only area where there was some comparability with other schools in the state. The other three variables illustrated how the selected schools for this study were significantly higher in socioeconomic status and had less impact from students with English language deficits.

California Learning Assessment System (CLAS)

The California Learning Assessment System (CLAS) was the standardized testing program utilized to select the schools for this study. CLAS began implementation in California during the 1992-93 school year. When evaluating and reporting school-level results, it included in its final report an analysis of the four specific demographic variables. The demographic information was obtained when the tests were administered to students.

The CLAS test became a center of controversy after the initial tests were administered in 1992-93 but did not reach a critical stage until the 1993-94 test administration. Many parents, as well as a number of educators, were not ready for this shift in assessment from predominantly multiple-choice responses with only one correct answer, to a review of a student's actual work samples where various interpretations could be made about what was the "correct" answer. Some of the criticism was valid to the degree that at the upper-grade levels, specifically in grades eight and ten, some of the questions asked in literature and social studies had an ideological perspective and could have skewed the results. (See Appendix B.)

The 1992-93 test administration was, in general, less of a problem than the 1993-94 test, mainly because parents were not aware of the content. There was little, if any, controversy regarding questions at the elementary level. The results at the elementary level were valid to the degree that enough students completed the test. All of the 18 schools that were included in this study had statistically valid test scores. In fact, the State Department of Education reported that over 96% of the schools in California had statistically valid test scores.

To attest to its effectiveness, a panel of experts was formed to review the entire testing program. Although they found the CLAS to be valid and reliable, several recommendations were made for subsequent assessment programs. In summary, the CLAS was judged to be an assessment program and was a valid measure of student achievement. It met the reasonable standard for a valid measurement instrument for student achievement; however, due to the controversy, a revised California student assessment system is under development.

Criteria for School Types

As indicated earlier, the school sites were selected from a comparison group of 100 schools (Appendix C). In order for higher-scoring schools to be compared to lower-scoring schools, a selection standard had to be established. The CLAS test reported scores at the fourth grade level in Reading, Language, and Math. In each of the subject areas there were six performance levels, which ranged from one being the lowest level of competence and six being the highest level of competence. Each of these subject areas was reported by indicating the percent of students who scored at each of the six performance levels.

The total percentage of scores in all three subject areas that were above level three were calculated for all of the schools in the band. They ranged from a high of 189%, scoring at level three and above to a low of 61%, scoring at level three and above. The standard used for selection for the high-scoring schools (Type I) was 150% and above, and the standard for lower performing schools (Type II) was 95% and below (Appendix D). These standards were set after a careful analysis of the scoring trends within the 100-school band. The majority of the schools in the band were clustered around the 120% range, and noticeable differences only began to show above 150% and below 95%.

Data Collection

The questionnaires were distributed to the 24 schools via the U.S. mail in April 1994. Returned questionnaires were checked for completion and usability, and then were entered into a computer file. This was completed and the results were tabulated in July 1994. Questionnaires were sent to the top 12 scoring schools and the lowest 12 scoring schools in the 100-school band selected from the California Learning Assessment System (CLAS). The percentage of students scoring 150% and above level three dropped off substantially after the top 12 schools. There was a similar drop-off of students scoring 95% and below level three at the bottom 12 schools. The entire administrative process, in most cases, took no more than 15 to 20 minutes. The completed questionnaires were collected by a teacher or administrator at each school site, placed in a sealed envelope, and returned via the U.S. mail.

All responses were kept confidential; however, a summary of the research was sent to all school sites that participated in the project if they requested that information. The questionnaires were anonymous and an identification number was affixed to each questionnaire that identified the school site. Names of individuals, as well as schools, were not used in the final text of the report. There was no attempt to make a comparison of individual schools. Participants were made aware of this factor in anticipation of them being more willing to take part in a study that would not individually compare their schools with other schools.

A response was received from 19 of the 24 schools; however, only 18 schools were analyzed for the final study. This was due to the fact that one of the respondent schools from Type I schools had only 4 out 23 teachers respond, and consequently the data was not usable. Five other schools refused to participate in the study; consequently, there was no data to analyze other than some limited demographic data of the principals. The six schools that did not participate in the study were demographically similar to the 18 participant schools because of the sampling procedures that focused on a 100-school band. The principal characteristics in these non-participating schools were also very similar. Four of the non-participation schools were Type I and two were Type II. Due to these strong demographic similarities, the non-participation of the six additional schools should not have had any significant impact on the outcomes of this study. (See Table 1.)

For those 18 schools participating in the study, 380 questionnaires were distributed. Out of these 380 questionnaires, 267 were returned, which resulted in a 70% return rate from those selected schools. It is interesting to note that it took numerous follow-up calls to most schools in the sample to get them to respond. The principals at schools that refused to participate stated various reasons such as not having enough time to administer the questionnaire, teachers were "already too tired," content of the questionnaire could be controversial, school was having contract negotiation problems and teachers were refusing to do "anything extra."

Although 6 out of 24 schools did not participate, the overall rate of participation was still 75%. One of the reasons for this high rate of participation may have been the effort made to convince principals to participate. It was a technique that may be of value to others who attempt survey research and therefore worthy of mention. On the information packet sent to school principals, a personal handwritten note was attached asking for their assistance. Clipped to the note were two one-dollar bills with a message to buy themselves a cup of cappuccino to reward them for their efforts to distribute the surveys. That was mentioned by several principals as being a clever way to get them to respond. (Note: All but one of the non-participating schools returned the two dollars with their questionnaires.)

Additional data related to the principal such as gender, ethnicity, number of years' teaching experience, number of years of administrative experience, and number of years in administration at current site was also collected. Neither principals nor other employees responded to the questionnaire. Principals were asked only to request that the survey be administered, and to supply basic demographic information about each of their school sites as well as themselves.

Pilot Study

A pilot study to test the administration of the questionnaires was conducted in December 1993 at an elementary school site in Ventura County. The school consisted of 560 students, 20 teachers, and one administrator. It was a school that was perceived by most parents, teachers, and administrators to be effective and consisting of a positive school climate.

The questionnaires were administered after a staff meeting per the recommended format (Appendix A). It took no more than 15 minutes total to read the directions to the staff, complete all questions, and collect all of the material from the teachers. The principal reported that teachers felt all questions were clear, as were the directions. There was, however, some minor confusion experienced with the Trust in Principal Scale. Some questions were marked with the asterisk signifying to "score in reverse." They were a distracter because some teachers thought they were to be answered in a different manner. The asterisks and adjoining statement about scoring in reverse were not included in the final draft of the Trust in Principal Scale.

All 20 of the teachers in the pilot school responded. Although the responses of only 20 teachers could not be considered to be a large enough sampling for any scholarly purposes, it did give some interesting data to "play with" prior to the final data collection. The development of this initial data matrix also gave the opportunity to set up the data in an organized manner that assisted in the reporting procedures for the final draft of the dissertation.

The Principal Behavior Scale was numbered 1-20 and the Trust in Principal Scale was numbered 21-27. As noted, each question was evaluated with the maximum and minimum score, the mean, and the standard deviation reported.

The Pearson Product Moment Correlation Matrix was the primary tool used for analysis. Correlations were tabulated analyzing the four principal behavioral constructs and how they related to the score on faculty trust. They ranged from 0.461 to 0.882, with the highest correlation between Praising and Buffering (0.882) and ranging down to the correlation between Caring and Involving (0.461). The correlations between faculty trust and the four principal behavior constructs were not as strong; however, they would still be considered noticeable. They were as follows:

Trust and Buffering   (0.534)
Trust and Involving   (0.383)
Trust and Praise   (0.334)
Trust and Caring   (0.262)

The pilot administration indicated that the questions were clear, and that the procedures were simple and efficient. The reporting format selected from the SYSTAT software program proved to be clear and concise.

Data Analysis and Reporting

The study used two data sources: (a) perceptual data from teachers regarding their principals behaviors and levels of faculty trust gathered through the use of questionnaires; and (b) scores on the standardized test required by the State Department of Education for students at grades 4, 8, and 10 (California Learning Assessment System). The SYSTAT (1989) computer software program was utilized, and a master file with all variables was created. The data was tabulated by case number and survey question. There were 267 case entries for each of the 20 questions on the Principal Behavior Scale and the seven questions on the Trust in Principal Scale. The data was reported as minimum and maximum scores, as well as standard deviations. It was also reported as a Pearson Product Moment Correlation Coefficient, as well as a t-test. Demographic data related to principals was also analyzed and reported.

The two questionnaires were administered to participant teachers. The first questionnaire was the Principal Behavior Scale (Appendix E), which attempted to measure these four principal behaviors. A 6-point Likert scale was constructed that measured the four specified principal behaviors (Praising, Buffering, Involving, and Caring). Each of these four specified principal behaviors was measured independently, and then correlated with the seven-statement Trust in Principal Scale (Appendix F). The Principal Behavior Scale had 20 total statements relating to principal behaviors. A total of 267 respondents ratings were tabulated for each of the 27 statements. Each statement was given a numerical weighting from 1-6 and the mean scores were analyzed as a total sample, as well as by the two school types. The maximum and minimum scores for each statement were reported, as well as the mean, range, and standard deviation.

There were five statements in each of the four behavior categories. The five statements were systematically sequenced so that they would be evenly distributed throughout the survey. When conducting the correlations between the variables each of the four principal behaviors was scored as an aggregate. For example, the five statements related to Buffering (2, 6, 10, 14, and 18) were analyzed based on the responses of all teachers and were reported as a mean score based on the same 1-6 scale. Each of the four principal behavioral constructs were reported as a scaled score (1-6), as well as with a minimum, maximum, and standard deviation. The four behavioral constructs were analyzed as a total sample, as well as by the two school types.

The second questionnaire was the seven question Trust in Principal Scale developed by Hoy and Kupersmith (1985). It had a 6-point Likert scale that required teachers to respond along a continuum from "strongly agree" to "strongly disagree." It was field tested, used in a number of studies, and found to be both reliable and valid. It was based on three sets of items developed to measure the components of faculty trust as defined by the conceptual framework and was based on a review of the literature. There were actually three independent scales that measured different areas of faculty trust:

1. Trust in Principal: Measures faculty confidence in the principal that he/she will keep his/her word and will act with the best interest of teachers in mind.

2. <u>Trust in Colleagues</u>: Measures faculty belief that they can depend on each other in difficult situations, and rely on the integrity of their colleagues.

3. <u>Trust in Organization</u>: Measures faculty belief that they can trust the school district to act in its best interest and to be fair to teachers.

The focus of this current research was on trust between the principal and faculty; consequently, only scale 1. <u>Trust in Principal</u> was utilized in this study.

To validate this instrument, Hoy and Kupersmith (1985) subjected each scale to a factor analysis. In each case, only one factor emerged with all items loading on that factor at a .6 or higher, supporting the unidimensionality of each scale. Each of the measures was checked for reliability, and alpha coefficients were found to be .93, .93, and .82, respectively. A validity check was also made correlating responses to global questions designed to measure each aspect of trust. The three scales (principal, colleagues, school district) correlated .94, .90, and .64 with the respective global terms. The <u>Trust in Principal Scale</u> used in this study actually had the highest validity and reliability ratings of all three scales.

The <u>Principal Behavior Scale</u> was used for the first time in a research study. The draft was reviewed by the Dissertation Committee Chair, three principals, three teachers, and two doctoral candidates to check for clarity, as well as content reliability. After the draft was evaluated, the questionnaire was revised accordingly and prepared for distribution.

Limitations

The scope of this study was limited for two major reasons:

1. The admonition that has been heard countless times regarding the fact that most doctoral students "bite off more than they can chew"; therefore, the scope was purposely narrowed to very specific behaviors.

2. The unique opportunity to use a highly focused comparison sample of schools that were similar in socioeconomic status, student mobility, and the number of Limited English Proficient (LEP) students; therefore, it limited the sample to 18 schools.

The sample was drawn largely from upper-middle-class families and focused on elementary schools only. There was also an additional limitation based on the narrow definition of an "effective" school. By using only one measure of effectiveness, namely the California Learning Assessment System scores, the sample was even more focused. This limited selection criteria was utilized in order to make the sample selection as narrow and objective as possible.

There was also a methodological limitation regarding the ability to compare aggregate data from 18 different school sites. There is a unique pattern of behavior and interactions with principals at each school that could make the perceptual data from schools inconsistent across school site boundaries. What one staff may perceive as Trust, Caring, Involving, Praising, and Buffering may be different from another. The focus was on the aggregate scores of the 267 respondents and how they viewed the 18 subject principals. No attempt was made to compare individual schools. This seems to be a limitation in any study that attempts to extrapolate information from a large sample that includes a number of sub-groups within that sample.

These limitations are found in similar research and were sufficiently mitigated by working very closely with the Dissertation Committee Chair and other Committee Members. These limitations were not significant enough to warrant any major modifications to the methodology, design, instruments, or sample population used in this study. It was apparent, however, that the Principal Behavior Scale will be in need of further refinement. A number of follow-up studies, as well as a factor analysis of the questionnaire, would be necessary to corroborate the instrument design and to determine its validity as well as reliability. This would be the case in any study utilizing a new measurement instrument.

CHAPTER FOUR

FINDINGS, ANALYSIS, AND DISCUSSION

Introduction

A number of variables were measured and analyzed in this study. The independent variables included the four principal behavior constructs, as well as other principal descriptive variables such as gender, ethnicity, number of years' teaching experience, number of years of administrative experience, and number of years at the school site. The dependent variable included the level of faculty trust in the principal.

The results of this study were based on the responses of 267 elementary school teachers. They were reported and analyzed as an aggregate of 18 schools, as well as broken down into two subgroups of 9 schools each. The subgroups included higher-scoring schools within the 100-school band and low-scoring schools within the same band. The raw data indicated that in a limited amount of cases not every question was answered in each of the questionnaires—thus, the total number of scores analyzed per question was not always consistent. When the data was broken down by school type, there were 127 respondents for school Type I (higher scoring) and 140 respondents for school Type II (lower scoring).

<u>Overview of Principals Demographics</u>

In total, 18 out of 24 principals participated in the study. Eight were male and 10 were female. There were only 2 ethnic minority principals and were identified as Afro-American. The 18 schools selected for the study were either K-5 or K-6. The 6 principals who did not participate included two male and four female. (See Table 1.)

The number of licensed staff per school site ranged from 9 to 27 teachers at each school site. The mean number of years' teaching experience for principals was 11.5, with a minimum of 4 years and a maximum of 23 years. The mean number of years' administrative experience was 11.9 years, with minimum of 4 years and a maximum of 26 years. The site level experience for the 18 principals was much less, with a mean of 5.3 years, a minimum of 1 year, and a maximum of 14 years.

The comparison figures in both school Type I and school Type II were very closely aligned. School Type 1 had 5 male and 4 female principals, whereas school Type II had 3 male and 6 female principals. Both school Type I and school Type II had 8 Anglo principals and only 1 Afro-American principal. The mean number of years teaching in school Type I was 11.5 years compared to 11.4 years in school Type II. The minimum number of years of teaching in school Type I was 5 years and the maximum was 21 years. In school Type II, the minimum number of years of teaching was 4 years and the maximum was 23 years.

The mean number of years' administrative experience in school Type I was 13.4 years compared to 10.5 years in school Type II. The minimum years of administrative experience in school Type I was 4 years and the maximum was 26 years. In school Type II, the minimum was 4 years and the maximum was 25 years. In school Type I, the mean site experience was 5.4 years and in school Type II it was 5.2 years. The minimum site level experience in school Type I was 2 years and the maximum was 15 years. In school Type II, the minimum was 1 year and the maximum was 12 years.

The only variable that indicated any substantial mean difference between the two school types was the number of years of administrative experience. Principals in school Type I had on the average 3 more years of experience than principals in school Type II. The mean number of years' teaching and mean number of years at the site level were closely matched at both types of schools.

The principal descriptive/demographic variables inclusive of gender, years of experience teaching, years of experience in administration, and years of experience at school site were analyzed to determine if there were significant factors effecting levels of faculty trust. The analysis indicated that none of these descriptive/demographic variables were substantially different among the 18 sample principals; in fact, they were strikingly similar. This would indicate that the demographic variables in this study would not be a significant factor in effecting the outcomes of this study.

This finding was supported by Cheng (1994) in a study of principal leadership, which indicated that there was no significant correlations between similar variables and the strength of principal leadership. Leitner (1994) also found this to be the case in correlating principal descriptive/demographic variables and student achievement. The principal behaviors that Leitner did find to effect student achievement were high principal visibility, rewarding teachers for their efforts, and enforcing high expectations for students.

Overview of Questionnaire Responses (N = 267)

The lowest overall mean score on the Trust in Principal Scale was 4.854 for Question T-5, "Teachers in this school often question the motives of the principal." The highest overall mean was 5.399 (6 = strongly disagree) on Question T-1, "The teachers in this school are suspicious of most of the principal's actions." This resulted in a range of 0.545 between the highest- and lowest-scoring questions on this seven-question scale. The range of responses within the individual questions on this questionnaire was generally 4.0 to 5.0.

The lowest overall mean score for all respondents ($\underline{N}$ = 267) on the Principal Behavior Scale was 3.714 for Question B-5, "Teachers in this school are recognized in award ceremonies." (Appendix G). The highest overall mean score was 5.300 for

Question B-20, "The principal really cares about the general well-being of the entire staff." This resulted in a range of 1.586 between the highest- and lowest-scoring questions on this 20-question scale. The range of responses within the individual questions on this questionnaire was generally 4.0 to 5.0 (6-point Likert scale).

The lowest standard deviation (SD) related to principal behaviors was 0.885 for Question B-15, "Teachers in this school are given a wide range of responsibilities by the principal." The highest SD was 1.425 for Question B-1, "Teachers in this school receive letters and notes praising their actions, from the principal." The lowest SD related to faculty trust was 0.863 for Question T-7, "The principal in this school keeps his/her word." The highest SD was 1.244 for Question T-5, "Teachers in this school often question the motives of the principal."

Analysis of Mean Scores for Questionnaire Responses (N = 267)

Principal Behavior Scale

In reviewing the results of the questionnaire responses for the Principal Behavior Scale, the lowest mean score was 3.71 for Question B-5, "Teachers in this school are recognized at award ceremonies." (See Appendix G.) The next lowest mean score was 4.33 for Question B-1, "Teachers in this school receive letters and notes praising their actions, from the principal." Both responses suggested that there was less formal recognition of teachers evidenced when compared to the other principal behaviors in the sample schools. The higher mean score of 4.94 for Question B-13, "Teachers in this school receive nonverbal praise such as smiles, handshakes, and pats on the back from the principal," suggested that what praising behaviors did take place by principals were usually informal gestures. It is significant to note that the two lowest mean scores on the entire questionnaire were questions categorized to be Praising behaviors.

The highest mean score was 5.30 for Question B-20, "The principal really cares about the general well-being of the entire staff." The next highest mean score was 5.25 for Question B-12, "Teachers in this school try new ideas and programs." Both responses indicated that respondents in the sample schools viewed the principal as showing genuine care about teachers, as well as encouraging them to try new ideas. It is significant to note that the two highest mean scores on the questionnaire were questions categorized to be <u>Caring</u> behaviors.

This finding was consistent with Johnston and Venable's (1986) study that found that elementary teachers responded more to a personal relationship of consideration with the principal rather than the involvement in decision making. Treslan and Ryan (1986) also found that teachers were more responsive to a principal's attempts to influence based on human relation skills, rather than use of hierarchical authority. Foster (1991) gave further support to the importance of caring in stating that administrators could actually transform school cultures by displaying inclusion (involving) as well as caring behaviors. Foster went on to say that successful principals were effective because of their personal and moral presence, their sense of "what's right," and their attention to people's needs.

The remainder of the questions on this questionnaire had mean scores that ranged from 4.41 for Question B-18, "Teachers in this school are asked to do a fair amount of paperwork," to 5.20 for Question B-15, "Teachers in this school are given a wide range of responsibilities by the principal." The fact that the majority of these 20 questions related to these principals' behaviors were scored at 4.70 and above on a 6.0 scale suggests that overall these four principal behavioral constructs were routinely observed by the sample respondents. This clearly illustrates the fact that principals found in this sample were viewed as being highly supportive of teachers. The only factor that could be remotely construed as a lack of support would be the limited use of "formal" praise of teachers in ceremonies.

Principal Behavioral Constructs (N = 267)

The highest mean score for the principal behavioral constructs were 5.01 for the <u>Involving</u> behaviors. (See Table 2.) This suggested that there was a significant level of teacher consultation, as well as site-based decision making, taking place among the sample respondents. The mean score of 4.98 for <u>Caring</u> behaviors also seems to indicate that genuine concern for teachers was being exhibited by principals. The mean score of 4.89 for <u>Buffering</u> behaviors also indicated that there were significant amounts of these supportive behaviors. The fact that the 4.56 score for <u>Praising</u> behavior was somewhat lower than the other three behaviors again suggests that it was the least significant of all the principal behaviors. This may have been due the fact that there was less formal <u>Praising</u> behavior taking place, such as public recognition at ceremonies. There were, however, some stronger indications of informal praising taking place.

Table 2

<u>Mean Scores of Behavioral Constructs</u>

Behavioral Constructs	Mean Scores[a]
Trust	5.277
Involving	5.017
Caring	4.982
Buffering	4.875
Praising	4.566

<u>Note.</u> Total sample = 18 schools.
[a]<u>N</u> = 267 total respondents.

This finding regarding <u>Praising</u> was not consistent with a previous study by Blase and Kirby (1992), which found that the most frequently reported behavior of principals to effect loyalty and trust was the use of Praise. It was, however, consistent with findings by Greenfield (1987), who noted that the use of praise to effect employee behavior may seem obvious but actually has very little research to support its impact. This does not seek to minimize the positive effects of authentic Praising behaviors. The research indicates that when praising is viewed as genuine, it is an important tool to be utilized by principals and should be a part of a repertoire of behaviors for improving school climate.

The four principal behavioral constructs were highly represented, with all four constructs having a mean score of 4.56 and above. The mean score of 5.27 for Trust was somewhat higher than those scores for the principal behavioral constructs, which ranged from 5.01 for Involving to 4.56 for Praising and suggests that Trust in the principal was highly evidenced among sample respondents.

Trust in Principal Scale

In reviewing the results of these questionnaire responses for the Trust in Principal survey, the lowest mean score was 4.85 for Question T-5, "Teachers in this school often question the motives of the principal." The next lowest was 5.24 for Question T-4, "The principal in this school typically acts with the best interest of teachers in mind." These were relatively high mean scores and they seem to suggest a significant level of trust in principals among sample respondents. The highest means score was 5.40 (strongly disagree) for Question T-1, "The teachers in this school are suspicious of most of the principal's actions." The next highest was 5.39 (strongly disagree) for Question T-3, "The principal takes unfair advantage of teachers in this school." Again, both questions suggested that there was a significant level of trust in the principal found among the respondents in this study.

The remainder of questions on this questionnaire had mean scores that ranged from 5.30 for Question T-6, "Teachers in this school trust the principal," to 5.37 for Question T-2, "Teachers in this school have faith in the integrity of the principal." The fact that on a 6.0 scale of Trust, five out of six questions had a 5.20

score or above, suggested that overall there was a relatively strong indication of faculty trust in the principal.

Analysis of Means by School Type

School Type I (n = 127)

The lowest mean score for the <u>Principal Behavior Scale</u> in school Type I was 3.806 for Question B-5; this question also had the highest <u>SD</u> at 1.733, "Teachers in this school are recognized in award ceremonies." The highest mean score was 5.476 for Question B-12; this question also had the lowest <u>SD</u> at 0.712, "Teachers in this school try new ideas and programs." This resulted in a range of 1.670 between the highest- and lowest-scoring questions on this 20-question scale.

The lowest mean score in the <u>Trust in Principal Scale</u> was 4.922 for Question T-5; this question also had the highest <u>SD</u> at 1.277, "Teachers in this school often question the motives of the principal." The highest mean score was 5.523 (6 = strongly disagree) for Question T-1, "The teachers in this school are suspicious of most of the principal's actions." The lowest <u>SD</u> was 0.832 for Question T-7, "The principal in this school keeps his/her word." This resulted in a range of 0.601 between the highest- and lowest-scoring questions on this seven-question scale.

Out of the four principal behavior constructs, the lowest mean score was 4.676 in <u>Praising</u>, with the highest <u>SD</u> = 0.995, and the highest mean score was 5.138 in <u>Involving</u>, with the lowest <u>SD</u> = 0.692. The mean score for <u>Buffering</u> was 4.928, the score for <u>Caring</u> was 5.110, and the mean score for <u>Trust</u> was 5.352.

School Type II (n = 140)

The lowest mean score for the <u>Principal Behavior Scale</u> in school Type II was 3.630 for Question B-5, "Teachers in this school are recognized in award ceremonies." The highest mean score was 5.113 for Question B-15; this question also had the lowest <u>SD</u> at 0.986, "Teachers in this school are given a wide range of responsibilities by the principal." The highest <u>SD</u> was 1.524 for Question B-18, "Teachers in this school feel that they are asked to do a fair amount of paperwork." This resulted in a range of 1.483 between the highest- and lowest-scoring questions on this 20-question scale.

The lowest mean score in the Trust in Principal Scale was 4.793 for Question T-5; this question also had the highest SD at 1.214, "Teachers in this school often question the motives of the principal." The highest mean score was 5.371 for Question T-7; this question also had the lowest SD at 0.895, "The principal in this school keeps his/her word." This resulted in a range of 0.578 between the highest- and lowest-scoring questions on this seven-question scale.

Out of the four principal behavior constructs the lowest mean score was 4.466 in Praising (highest SD = 1.008) and the highest was 4.909 for Involving. The mean score for Buffering was 4.826, with the lowest SD at 0.938. The score for Caring was 4.866, and the mean score for Trust was 5.208. (See Table 3.)

Comparison of School Type I and II

Although the two different school types identified for this study were not significantly different, there were some variations in standardized test scores. The California Learning Assessment System (CLAS) scores were slightly higher in school Type I than those in school Type II; however, in general the scores in both school types were indicative of relatively high-performance schools.

In both school Type I and II, the lowest mean score was again related to Question B-5, "Teachers in this school are recognized at award ceremonies." The mean score in school Type I was 3.80, and in school Type II the mean score was 3.63. The highest mean score in school Type I was 5.48 for question B-12, "Teachers in this school try new ideas and programs." In school Type II, the highest mean score was 5.11 for Question B-15, "Teachers in this school are given a wide range of responsibilities by the principal." This suggested that teachers in the total sample felt comfortable in trying new approaches and were given some level of shared responsibilities. The lowest mean score in both school Type I and II was in the area of Praising and the highest in the area of Caring. This was identical to the findings in the aggregate sample of 18 schools.

Table 3

Mean Scores and Standard Deviations of Behavioral Constructs by School Type

Behavioral Constructs	School Type I[a]	SD	School Type IIb	SD
Trust	5.352	.709	5.20	.853
Involving	5.138	.692	4.909	.953
Caring	5.110	.778	4.866	1.006
Buffering	4.928	.794	4.826	.938
Praising	4.676	.996	4.466	1.008

Note. Total sample = 18 schools
a_n = 127 respondents
b_n = 140 respondents

In both school types, the lowest mean score for the principal behavioral constructs was in the Praising behaviors. In school Type I the mean score was 4.68, and in school Type II it was 4.47. In both school types the highest mean score was in the area of Involving behaviors. In school Type I the mean score was 5.14 and in school Type II the mean score was 4.91. This again supported the finding that the principal's use of Praising behavior was more limited than the other three principal behaviors. It also indicated that involving teachers in decision making was a characteristic found in both types of schools.

The lowest mean score in both school types in the area of Trust was Question T-5, "Teachers in this school often question the motives of the principal." The mean score in school Type I was 4.92 and in school Type II it was 4.79. This low mean score indicated that teachers generally viewed the principal's behavior as being trustworthy. In school Type I, the highest mean score was 5.52 (strongly disagree) for Question T-1, "Teachers in this school are suspicious of most of the principal's actions." The scores indicated that there was very little suspicion of the principal's actions. The highest mean score in school Type II was 5.24 for Question T-6, "Teachers in this school trust the principal." In school Type I the overall mean score for Trust was 5.35, and in school Type II the mean score was 5.21. These high mean scores suggest that there is strong faculty Trust in the principal in both school types.

There was a higher mean score for Caring and Involving behaviors among respondents in school Type I. This higher level of Caring and Involving behaviors in school Type I may indicate that principals had more of a willingness to utilize these types of behaviors in schools that were considered to be more effective.

The consistent finding was that all four principal behaviors, as well as faculty Trust, were highly evidenced in both school types. The Praising behaviors were not as significant as the other behaviors; however, they were still evidenced to some degree. In general, the mean scores between the school types were similar and what variations did occur were not highly significant.

Testing the Hypotheses

The Pearson Product-Moment Correlation Coefficient was used to measure the strengths of association between the major variables. This was defined as the covariance of variable X and Y divided by the product of the standard deviation of X and the standard deviation of Y. It described the linear relationship between the variables of trust and the four principal behavior constructs. It takes on values from -1.00 to +1.00, where the magnitude provides an index of strength and the sign an index of direction. Alpha levels of significance were determined and also reported through utilizing the SYSTAT computer software program.

There are various interpretations of what constitutes a significant coefficient (r) correlation. For purpose of this study, the standard of analysis reported by Best (1981, p. 255) was utilized. It is as follows:

Coefficient (r)	Relationship
.00 to .20	negligible
.20 to .40	low
.40 to .60	moderate
.60 to .80	substantial
.80 to 1.00	high to very high

The threshold standard was set at .50 and above. The correlation was not considered to be meaningful unless it attained this level.

Analysis of Pearson Correlations (N = 267)

The Pearson Correlations for all five major variables in the study, inclusive of the four principal behavioral constructs and of faculty trust, were all significantly correlated at the "moderate" to "substantial" range. The highest correlation of .725 was found between <u>Buffering</u> and <u>Trust</u>, and the lowest of .567 was found between <u>Praising</u> and <u>Trust</u>. This included the finding that there was a high correlation among all four principal behavioral constructs as well. The highest correlation of .738 was found between <u>Buffering</u> and <u>Involving</u>, and the lowest of .613 was found between <u>Buffering</u> and <u>Praising</u>. The correlations among these five variables were also calculated to be at the .01 level of significance.

It is important to note that the four principal behaviors were highly correlated among themselves. This high correlation among the principal behavioral constructs suggests that they may not be as distinctly different behaviors as was postulated. While the data indicates that there was indeed a group of principal behaviors that were highly correlated with levels of faculty trust in the principal, it also indicated that these four principal behaviors were difficult to measure as separate behavioral constructs because they were so highly correlated.

This finding supports the notion that there may be a "behavioral cluster," rather than four different behaviors, that was actually being measured. This would indicate a need to further refine the instrument so that these behaviors could be measured more efficiently. Perhaps a more realistic view would be that these four behavioral constructs were so interrelated that they could not be measured separately. If this were the case, a new measuring instrument would have to be developed that would not attempt to measure such specifically defined behaviors as separate constructs.

The fact is, however, that these four principal behavioral constructs, either separately or collectively, were significantly correlated with levels of faculty trust in the principal. The notion that a principal's behavior is significantly related to the establishment of levels of trust is a powerful one. This is especially important when considering that a direct correlation was found in previous studies by Heck et al. (1990), Hoy et al. (1990), Hoy et al. (1991), and Bossert et al. (1982) linking a principal's behavior to student achievement. This connection between a principal's behavior and levels of faculty trust is a key finding, especially when considering the correlations for all five variables were calculated at the .01 level of significance.

Analysis of Pearson Correlations for School Type I and II

The fact that the correlations for all variables were somewhat higher at school Type II than school Type I may have indicated that those specific principal behaviors had a more powerful effect on faculty trust at these lower-scoring Type II schools. One could speculate that based on these results that a principal's behavior had more influence at the lower-achieving schools than the higher-achieving schools because the teachers may have been more responsive to this type of supportive leadership. At the higher-achieving Type I schools, there may have been less of a need for the principal to exhibit these types of behaviors, simply because the teachers did not need as much administrative support. At these Type I schools, teachers may gain enough support from the high rate of success they experience in the classroom and do not need the same amount of "moral" support from the principal as may be needed in lower-performing schools.

The most illustrative example of the difference in school types was in the correlation between the Buffering and Trusting behaviors. In school Type I the Pearson Correlation was .643, and for school Type II it was .776. This was the widest margin of all of the correlations among the major variables between the two schools. This suggests that the principal's intervention to "protect" or buffer teachers from negative outside influences has a more powerful effect on levels of trust at the lower-achieving Type II schools than the higher-achieving Type I schools.

The lowest correlations were .490 for <u>Praising</u> behaviors in school Type I and .618 for <u>Praising</u> behaviors in school Type II. This supports the notion that this <u>Praising</u> behavior did not have the same impact as other supportive behaviors, particularly in the higher-achieving Type I schools. This finding was consistent in regard to <u>Praising</u> behaviors not only being less demonstrated by principals, but also having a weaker correlation with levels of faculty <u>Trust</u> than the other three principal behaviors. It is important to note that these <u>Praising</u> behaviors did seem to have more of an effect at the lower-achieving Type II schools than the higher-achieving Type I schools; the difference was not statistically significant.

Overview of Pearson Product Moment Correlation Coefficients

The Pearson correlations for the five major variables were moderate to substantial and were calculated at .01 level of significance.

There were also very strong correlations among the four principal behavioral constructs. The highest was between <u>Buffering</u> and <u>Involving</u> (0.738) and the lowest between <u>Buffering</u> and <u>Praising</u> (0.613). All of the principal behaviors, however, were highly correlated among themselves and calculated at the .01 level of significance. (See Table 4.) The Pearson Product Moment Correlation Coefficient was used to analyze Hypotheses One and Two, and an independent <u>t</u>-test was used to analyze Hypothesis Three.

Hypothesis One

There are specific and observable principal behaviors that are correlated with levels of faculty trust.

The questions for the first hypothesis were: Do the scores on the Principal Behavior Scale have a direct positive correlation with the scores on the Trust in Principal Scale? Were there any negative correlations?

This hypothesis was supported. There was a "substantial" to "moderate" Pearson Correlation between all four principal behavioral constructs and levels of faculty trust. The fact that they were all correlated at .567 or better indicated a strong association between these variables. These were all significant at the .01 level.

Table 4

Pearson Correlations between Trust/Behavioral Constructs

	Trust	Caring	Buffering	Involving	Praising
Caring	0.715	1.000			
Buffering	0.725	0.640	1.000		
Involving	0.645	0.702	0.738	1.000	
Praising	0.567	0.721	0.613	0.642	1.000

Note. Total sample = 18 schools. $\underline{N}$ = 267 total respondents.

The data also indicated that the correlations were positive in direction. The surveys were constructed so that the larger the numerical score, the more positive the response. In general, it could be stated that these "substantial" to "moderate" correlations indicated that the four principal behaviors had a significant impact on levels of faculty trust. There were no negative correlations.

The principal behavioral constructs were also highly correlated among themselves, which suggested that the principal behaviors themselves were very much interrelated. With these high correlations among them, it is not clear if these four behavioral constructs were indeed measured as separate identifiable behaviors. Nevertheless, it was apparent that these four principal behaviors, individually or collectively, did have a positive effect on levels of faculty trust.

This finding was supported in a study by Hoy et al. (1978), which indicated that a principal's balanced use of "informal" and "formal" authority was most effective in creating a positive school climate and concurrent levels of Trust. The four principal behavioral constructs identified in this study would fall into the "informal authority" category of principal behavior. Hoy et al. also found that "consideration," defined as the ability of the principal to project concern, and "non-authoritarian" behavior were key components in establishing a positive school climate and concurrent levels of Trust. The term "consideration" in Hoy et al.'s study would be analogous to Caring behaviors and the term "non-authoritarian" to Involving behaviors. Hoy et al.'s finding in their study was consistent with this research and support the importance of a principal demonstrating genuine care and concern for teachers. The evidence seems to be consistent throughout this study, as well as documented in the review of the literature, that a principal's behavior can indeed effect the level of faculty trust, consequently school climate, and ultimately student performance.

Hypothesis Two

Some principal behaviors have more powerful effects on levels of faculty trust than others.

The question for the second hypothesis was as follows: Which, if any, of these four principal behaviors are more significantly correlated with faculty trust?

This hypothesis was supported. There was a "substantial" to "moderate" Pearson Correlation for all principal behavioral constructs and levels of faculty Trust. The highest correlation of .725 was found between Buffering behaviors and faculty Trust, the second-highest correlation of .715 was found between Caring and faculty Trust, and the third-highest correlation of

.645 was found between <u>Involving</u> and faculty <u>Trust</u>. The only principal behavioral construct that had a somewhat lower correlation was the <u>Praising</u> behaviors, which was correlated at .567 with faculty <u>Trust</u>.

In school Type I, the strongest correlation was 0.643 for <u>Buffering</u> behaviors and the lowest was 0.490 for <u>Praising</u> behaviors. This difference was fairly large and seemed to indicate that <u>Praising</u> behaviors did not have the same impacts on levels of trust. It indicated that the <u>Buffering</u> behaviors as well as the <u>Caring</u> behaviors at 0.637 and <u>Involving</u> at 0.607 had a greater effect on levels of faculty <u>Trust</u> than <u>Praising</u>.

In school Type II, <u>Buffering</u> behaviors also had the highest correlation with <u>Trust</u> at 0.776, and the <u>Praising</u> behaviors also had the lowest at 0.618. <u>Caring</u> was correlated at 0.757 and <u>Involving</u> at 0.663. Again, <u>Buffering</u>, <u>Caring</u>, and <u>Involving</u> behaviors had a more significant impact on faculty <u>Trust</u> than <u>Praising</u>. (See Table 5.)

The higher correlations found regarding the <u>Buffering</u> and <u>Caring</u> behaviors suggested that building <u>Trust</u> and improving school climate was more closely related to a principal's tending to a teacher's personal needs, rather than for recognizing a teacher's accomplishments. This is not to say that <u>Praise</u> was not a necessary ingredient in creating trust; it just did not seem to have the same impact as the other three principal behaviors. Another key finding in this study was the powerful effects of a principal <u>Caring</u> for a teacher's personal needs and genuine interest in their personal life. It suggests that among the most important leadership behaviors was the "human" aspect of a principal's behavior.

Table 5

Pearson Correlations between Trust and Behavioral Constructs by School Type

	Trust	Caring	Buffering	Involving	Praising
School Type I (n = 9)[a]					
Caring	0.537	1.000			
Buffering	0.643	0.537	1.000		
Involving	0.607	0.606	0.714	1.000	
Praising	0.490	0.630	0.635	0.645	1.000
School Type II (n = 9)[b]					
Caring	0.757	1.000			
Buffering	0.776	0.702	1.000		
Involving	0.663	0.744	0.755	1.000	
Praising	0.618	0.782	0.597	0.641	1.000

[a]127 respondents
[b]140 respondents

The fact that Type II schools had higher correlations than Type I schools for all variables suggests that those principal behaviors were more influential in Type II schools. This would lead one to speculate that these supportive principal behaviors were less necessary in the Type I schools, in part due to the high performance of students in the classroom. The teachers in the Type I schools may get enough support and satisfaction from the simple fact that they seem to have highly effective classrooms and students and may not need a high level of support from principals. The reverse may be true in Type II schools, where the lower performance of students may require more principal interventions and support.

Type II schools also had wider ranges in their responses to the questionnaire. The Standard Deviations for all variables were higher in Type II schools (see Table 3). The <u>SD</u> for <u>Trust</u> in Type I schools was calculated at .709, whereas the <u>SD</u> for <u>Trust</u> in Type II schools was .853. The remainder of the variables in Type II schools had higher <u>SD</u>s. They were as follows: <u>Praising</u>, 1.008; <u>Caring</u>, 1.006; <u>Involving</u>, .953; and <u>Buffering</u>, .938. The higher <u>SD</u>s in Type II schools may have contributed to the higher correlations of all five variables in Type II schools.

Sergiovanni (1984, p. 40) identified four leadership forces/behaviors to explain how leadership is related to school performance. These five behaviors included the following:

1. <u>Human</u>: supportive, caring, fosters participation.
2. <u>Political</u>: persuasive, builds alliances, solves conflicts.
3. <u>Symbolic</u>: inspirational, charismatic.
4. <u>Educational</u>: organization, professional development.

Up until this point, most "effective schools" research seems to have focused on the political, educational, and symbolic aspects of leadership. The results of this study suggest that emphasis on the "human" aspects of leadership may be more important than we have previously been led to believe in establishing an effective school.

This was consistent with the findings of Hoy et al. (1991), which indicated that "consideration" and "institutional integrity" were the best predictors of teachers having <u>Trust</u> in the principal. The terms "consideration" and "institutional integrity" were analogous to the terms <u>Caring</u> and <u>Buffering</u> in this current study. Hoy et al. (1990) also found that principals who were helpful and genuinely concerned about the welfare of their teachers were most likely to have the trust of their teachers and that 20% of the variance of faculty trust in the principal was attributed to the principal's supportiveness. Blase and Kirby (1992) also noted that principal "support" for teachers increased their confidence which, in turn, increased their effectiveness in the classroom. The concept of "support" is analogous to <u>Buffering</u> behaviors in the current study.

Hypothesis Three

Schools that are considered to be effective have higher levels of faculty trust than schools that are considered to be less effective.

The questions for the third hypothesis were: Do schools with higher achievement test scores have higher levels of faculty trust? Do schools with higher achievement test scores have principals who exhibit these principal behaviors more frequently?

This hypothesis was only partially supported. The t-test scores comparing faculty trust in principal at both school types resulted in findings that were not expected. These scores indicated that although the mean score for trust in school Type I was higher, they did not attain a level of significance. The alpha level of 0.136 did not meet the minimum standard of 0.05 level of significance. It is important to note, however, that the level of faculty trust in principal was high in both types of schools. (See Table 6.)

In order to analyze the third hypothesis, a t-test was conducted in order to make a comparison of school Type I and school type II. A one-tailed t-test was used because a comparison of groups was being made and there was a need to indicate direction. In other words, the hypothesis stated that one group would have significantly higher mean scores than another comparison group. In this case, the review of literature indicated that levels of faculty trust should be higher at the higher-performing Type I schools. In conducting a t-test, t must equal or exceed the t-critical value for the rejection of the null hypothesis. For a one-tailed test, since the 5% area of rejection is either at the upper tail or at the lower tail of the curve, the t-critical value should be lower. The t-critical value in this such case would be 1.645 (pooled variance). The pooled variance was used, rather than the separate variance, because the sample sizes were different. (See Table 6.)

Table 6

Independent Samples t-Test on Trust/Behavior
Constructs by School Type

Group n	M	SD
	Trust	
Type I	128	5.352	0.709
Type II	140	5.208	0.853

Separate Variances $\underline{t}$ = 1.507, df = 263.7, p = 0.133
Pooled Variances t = 1.494, df = 266, p = 0.136

	Caring	
Type I	127	5.110	0.778
Type II	141	4.866	1.006

Separate Variances $\underline{t}$ = 2.227, df = 260.2, p = 0.027
Pooled Variances t = 2.198, df = 266, p = 0.029

	Involving	
Type I	127	5.138	0.692
Type II	141	4.909	0.953

Separate Variances $\underline{t}$ = 2.266, df = 254.8, p = 0.024
Pooled Variances t = 2.230, df = 266, p = 0.027

Group n	M	SD
	Buffering	
Type I	128	4.928	0.794
Type II	141	4.826	0.938

Separate Variances $\underline{t}$ = 0.963, df = 265.7, p = 0.336
Pooled Variances t = 0.955, df = 267, p = 0.340

		Praising	
Type I	128	4.676	0.998
Type II	141	4.466	1.008

Separate Variances $t = 1.722$, df $= 265$, p $= 0.086$
Pooled Variances $t = 1.721$, df $= 267$, p $= 0.086$

There were, however, some significant differences in the principal behaviors between school Type I and school Type II. The mean score for <u>Caring</u> behaviors in school Type I was 5.110 and in school Type II it was 4.866. The probability of these differences being significant was 0.029, which was within the .05 level of significance. This was also the case in the area of <u>Involving</u> behaviors, where in school Type I the mean score was 5.138 and in school Type II it was 4.909. The probability of these differences being significant was 0.027, which was again within the .05 significance level.

The data did indicate a trend where the mean scores for all variables was higher in the "more effective" Type I schools than the "less effective" Type II schools. This would suggest that schools that had achievement tests that were significantly lower would more than likely have proportionate reductions in levels on all five major variables. Further study would be needed to support this assumption; however, it would be consistent with this research and the general findings in the review of the literature.

It is important to note that the term "effective" used in this study is a relative term. It was based on the 1993-94 CLAS test scores alone and, therefore, has a limited scope in defining an effective school. Overall, both school types had scores indicating a more than adequate level of academic achievement. Although the scores found in school Type II were lower, they were not necessarily indicative of "less effective" schools.

<u>Summary Analysis</u>

In summary, two out of the three hypotheses were supported. The first two hypotheses indicated that principals and their subsequent behaviors did seem to have significant impacts on the levels of faculty <u>Trust</u> in the principal, with <u>Buffering</u> behaviors having the most significant impact and <u>Praising</u> behaviors the least significant impact. The third hypothesis regarding the different levels of <u>Trust</u> attributed to the two school types was not supported. There were slightly higher scores for all variables in the higher-achieving school Type I; however, they were not statistically significant.

The evidence seems to be clear regarding the principals' ability to create an atmosphere of <u>Trust</u>. This is important to the degree that creating a positive environment is a critical factor in the establishment of an effective school. A team effort, which in turn lays the groundwork for better communication and more coordinated efforts to provide instruction, is the key to an effective school. The review of the literature, as well as the results of this study, have indicted a strong correlation between a principal's behavior and levels of faculty trust.

CHAPTER FIVE

CONCLUSIONS AND IMPLICATIONS FOR RESEARCH

Introduction

This study adds to our knowledge of what principals "do" in order to make their schools more effective. Convincing evidence has been offered that demonstrates that the level of faculty trust is highly correlated with principal behavior. The data suggests that traditional leadership behavior, such as hierarchical and top-down decision making, may be less effective than behaviors that establish an atmosphere where professional and collegial relations can flourish. Slater (1991) goes as far as to suggest that principals with personalities and leadership styles oriented toward hierarchical methods should consider a different managerial style or another position in education. The evidence from this study supports the notion that a principal can influence a teacher's perceptions. In other words, there seems to be a direct link between the principal's behavior and its effect on teacher attitudes regarding trust.

In-School Linkages

Wilson and Corbett (1983) state that principals can influence teacher behavior and instruction through "in-school linkages." There are three types of in-school linkages: cultural, structural, and interpersonal. The structural linkage mechanisms are supervision, evaluation, rules, procedures, plans, schedules, and vertical information systems. School cultural linkages are the norms and values personified in the unique rituals that influence teacher behavior. The interpersonal linkages promote greater knowledge of instructional strategies and increase the degree of inter-relatedness among staff. The principal behavioral constructs identified in this study are roughly equivalent to these cultural and interpersonal linkages.

Leitner (1994) used this concept to determine what linkages had more of an impact on student achievement. The results indicated that principals in high-achieving schools engaged in more behaviors associated with cultural linkages than any other of the linkages, although interpersonal linkages were also at a significant level. Principals in higher SES schools displayed more instructional management behavior than their counterparts in lower SES schools, especially in terms of defining the schools mission and promoting a positive school climate.

Impacts of Positive School Climate and Trust

Larson and LaFasto (1989) found that a climate of trust allowed staff members to function as an effective team. It allowed a faculty to stay problem focused and collaborative, and it promoted more efficient communication and coordination. It also improved the area of "compensation," where team members assisted one another in the completion of their tasks. This finding was perhaps the vital connection that links a positive school climate to increased student achievement. Trust can develop a positive school climate, a positive school climate can enhance the ability for a coordinated team effort through improved communication, and this improved communication and coordination can result in a more effective instructional program.

Land and Jarman (1992) have underscored the importance of Trust being a key factor in the most successful organizations in the business world. They even went as far as to say that the terms "trust" and "love" could be used interchangeably. They refer to statements by key executives noting the importance of Trust in their business organizations. For example, Jan Carlzon, president of Scandinavian Airlines System, states his philosophy in the following manner: "People are not willing to take risks when they feel afraid or threatened. But if you manage them by love—that is if you show them respect and trust—they start to perform up to their real capabilities" (p. 205). Robert Townsend of Avis Rent-a-Car offers another example: "The real essence of leadership is to care about your people" (p. 206).

Bossert et al. (1982) indicated that a principal's management behavior affects the social climate directly as well as the instructional organization in the school which, in turn, directly affect student learning. It is important to note that this was evident even after controlling for SES.

Hoy et al. (1991) perhaps best summarize this connection between a principal's supportive behavior and a healthy and positive school climate:

> The principal who is friendly, supportive, open and collegial in interactions with teachers is able to command their respect and trust, and trust is further enhanced by protecting teachers. The major explanation for the establishment of a climate of trust in the principal seems to arise from the behavior of the principal that is caring, collegial, supportive, and protective. (p. 112)

The data indicated that the notion of a leader who cares only about the task at hand or the end product, and is not concerned about the people in the organization, can no longer be an effective leader. The model leader in today's complex world is one who cares about the people in the organization first, and the product or service second. This does not minimize the need for a top-quality product or service; it is merely a recognition that this can only be accomplished through caring for, and working with, the people in the organization.

One of the principal behaviors that was most strongly evidenced, <u>Caring</u>, was the general subject of the May 1995 <u>Phi Delta Kappan</u> magazine. The articles were presented in the context of the importance of providing a caring environment in the classroom; however, the point is that such an affective behavior has reached this level of importance that it is now the major theme of a mainstream education journal. If caring is viewed as such a crucial dynamic between teacher and student, it can be certainly said to be just as important to exist between principal and teacher.

Traditional training programs that may stress hierarchical management will need to be revised so that more time can be spent in developing methods to increase collegiality and levels of mutual trust. The four principal behaviors that have been the focus of this study (i.e., <u>Caring</u>, <u>Buffering</u>, <u>Involving</u>, and <u>Praising</u>) need to be incorporated into any effective training program for administrators.

Similar attempts have been made to measure leadership practices. Kouzes and Posner (1989) constructed a 30-question survey that measured principal behaviors in constructs they categorized as Challenging, Inspiring, Enabling, Modeling, and Encouraging behaviors. The "Leadership Practices Inventory" is a survey based on a 5-point scale that ranks leaders high, medium, and low in these categories. It is constructed as a self-evaluation tool, as well as a tool for employees to rank the behaviors of their supervisors. Kouzes and Posner (1990) found that when leaders score high in these areas, their organizations were seen as more effective because they were willing to share power by involving employees in decision making. They also found that these leaders set high expectations and modeled the type of behavior they expected by openly displaying the strength of their convictions.

<u>Implications for Further Research Study</u>

This research raises a number of important theoretical as well as application questions. More research needs to be done exploring this important relationship between the principal and faculty. A replication study of a lower functioning and/or lower SES group of schools would be of great interest to see if the same results would be found. An additional study on schools with much wider discrepancies in achievement test data would also be of value. Another area to explore would be to compare individual schools in a similar study and to focus on the interrelationships between the principal and faculty on a school-by-school comparison. This type of scrutiny of individual schools would require a more in-depth qualitative analysis, but it could perhaps shed more light on the dynamics between principal and faculty.

It would also be of interest to replicate this study in the private sector, as well as in other organizations, to see if there would be any variation. Would <u>Caring</u> behaviors have a weaker correlation at General Motors or IBM? Would <u>Involving</u> behaviors have a higher correlation in a large hospital setting? Would <u>Buffering</u> behaviors be found in a large urban police department? Would <u>Praising</u> behaviors be used more or less frequently at the secondary school level?

Perhaps one of the most important issues to revisit would be regarding the principal behaviors themselves and the attempts to isolate and measure them. The <u>Principal Behavior Scale</u> was used for the first time, and it is still not clear whether or not it measured what it was supposed to be measuring. Replication and subsequent refinement of this instrument would be a substantial contribution to research in the field of principal leadership.

<u>Application and Practice</u>

This research should be of use to practitioners who would like to improve school performance. If strong correlations have been made between specific principal behaviors and the establishment of higher levels of trust, we can begin to develop training programs for administrators so that they may acquire some of these necessary interpersonal leadership skills. The powerful impact of principals on the quality of education at a school site must be closely scrutinized. The connection between the principal as the leader of a school site to the student sitting in a classroom may be stronger and much more direct than we previously realized. The teacher has always been the major influence on students in the classroom; however, the principal's behavior may have more direct impact on instruction than we have previously thought.

Glasman and Nevo (1988) note that this linkage is a complex one because of the varied relationships between the principal's efforts and the teachers' efforts, as well as between the teachers' efforts and what students actually learn. They point out that there is still much ambiguity regarding what we mean by learning and what we define as an effective school despite the extensive research that has been conducted since the turn of the century. This, of course, is true, but we must also realize that there are definite impacts created by the principal that could profoundly change what happens in a classroom. A positive school environment seems to be a necessary component for a school to be successful, and this is one way a principal can directly impact the classroom. By establishing an atmosphere of mutual trust and cooperation in which effective instruction can be offered, the principal can make a difference.

It seems that a conceptual framework has been identified in this study. It illustrates a vital, although indirect, connection between principal behaviors and student performance. The data indicates a significant correlation between principal behaviors and faculty trust. The review of the literature has also indicated the importance of faculty trust and a positive school climate. There also seems to be a connection between fostering a positive school climate and student performance levels.

Although the intention of this study was merely to illustrate the connection between a principal's behaviors and the levels of faculty trust, there are other relationships that can be drawn. There seems to be an indirect connection between student performance and the establishment of trust and a positive school climate. The key relationship between trust and student outcomes appears to be the dynamic that allows for an atmosphere in which teachers can work in effective teams when open communication is present. (See Figure 1.)

Trust and Teamwork

Larson and LaFasto (1989) have identified Trust as one of those "mainstay virtues in the commerce of mankind" (p. 85).

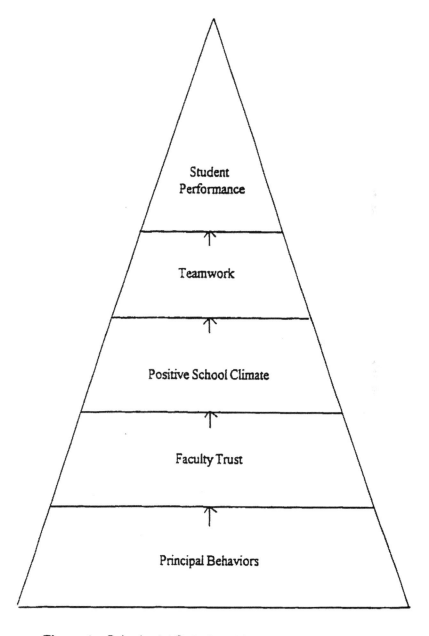

Figure 1. Principals' Relationship to Student Performance.

They go on to say that <u>Trust</u> can only be produced in a climate of honesty, openness, consistency, and respect. These, and similar findings, have strong implications in the development of principal leadership programs, as well as giving practicing administrators some guidance on where to focus their leadership skills.

They have identified four themes to help explain why a climate of trust assists in fostering teamwork:

1. Trust allows team members to stay problem focused; there are no hidden agendas to sidetrack group objectives.

2. Trust promotes more efficient communication and coordination; candidness ensures few misunderstandings.

3. Trust improves the quality of collaborative outcomes; group members are willing to take risks.

4. Trust leads to compensation; members will pick up the slack of a faltering team member.

This high level of trust allows teams to function with the following characteristics that describe a highly effective group in action: (a) a clear and elevating goal, (b) a results-driven structure, (c) competent members, (d) a unified commitment, (e) a collaborative climate, (f) standards of excellence, (g) external support and recognition, and (h) principled leadership.

This is another key connection made in this study. Feeling good about one's teaching environment is only as valuable as it makes one a more effective teacher. What is it about the positive school climate that makes a school more effective? It appears simply to be the fostering of teamwork and open communication that can occur in an atmosphere of trust.

Our public education system is in the beginning stages of a major paradigm shift. We need to know what is working and what isn't working to make our schools more effective. We need to know what principal behaviors to keep and which ones to leave behind. As we make this shift, we need to identify the leadership style that will cross this bridge into the future. It appears that the creation of an atmosphere of trust at a school site is important and within the power of the principal. With this climate of trust, the potential of working teams can be realized and the full power of learning unleashed.

Our public schools seem to be under attack from all quarters; however, the metaphor for the new effective schools and organizations should not be the military during times of battle. Rather, it should be that of a family unit taking care of one another's needs and making sure that their goals are accomplished while maintaining the family values of mutual trust and support. It is my hope that this research will add to the scholarly, as well as practical, body of knowledge that will be so essential in improving our public education system as we enter the twenty-first century.

REFERENCES

Ashforth, S. J. (1985). Climate formations: Issues and extensions. Academy of Management Review, 25, 837-847.

Azumi, J. E., & Madhere, S. (1983). Professionalism, power, and performance: The relationship between administrative control, teacher conformity, and student achievement. Paper presented at the annual meeting of the American Educational Research Association, Montreal.

Barnard, C. L. (1938). Functions of the executive. Cambridge, MA: Harvard University Press.

Bennis, W., & Nanus B. (1985). Leaders: The strategies for taking charge. New York: Harper & Row.

Best, J. W. (1981). Research in education. Englewood Cliffs, NJ: Prentice-Hall, Inc.

Bishop, J. M. (1977). Organizational influences on the work orientations of elementary teachers. Sociology of Work and Occupations, 4, 171-208.

Blase, J. J., & Kirby, P.C. (1992). <u>Bringing out the best in teachers: What effective principals do.</u> Newbury Park, CA: Corwin Press.

Blau, P. M., & Scott, W. R. (1962). <u>Formal organizations.</u> San Francisco: Chandler.

Blumberg. W., & Greenfield W. (1980). <u>The effective principal: Perspectives on school leadership.</u> Boston: Allyn & Bacon.

Bossert, S. T., Dwyer, D. C., Rowan, B., & Lee, G. V. (1982). The instructional management role of the principal. <u>Educational Administration Quarterly, 18,</u> 34-64.

Burns, J. M. (1978). <u>Leadership.</u> New York: Harper & Row.

Campbell, R. (1957). <u>Administrative behavior in education.</u> New York: Harper and Brothers.

Cheng, Y. C. (1994). Profiles of organizational culture and effective schools. <u>School Effectiveness and School Improvement, 4</u>(2), 85-110.

Coleman, J. S., Campbell, E. Q., Hobson, C. J., McPartland, J., Mood, A., Weinfield, F. D., & York, R. L. (1966). <u>Equality of educational opportunity.</u> Washington, DC: U.S. Government Printing Office.

Deal, T. (1987). Effective school principals: Counselors, engineers, pawn brokers, poets...or instructional leaders? In W. Greenfield (Ed.), <u>Instructional leadership: Concepts, issues, and controversies</u> (pp. 230-245). Boston: Allyn & Bacon.

Edmonds, R. (1979). Effective schools for the urban poor. <u>Educational Leadership, 37,</u> 15-24.

Etzioni, A. (1975). <u>A comparative analysis of complex organizations.</u> New York: Free Press.

Foskett, J. (1967). <u>The normative world of the elementary school principal.</u> Eugene: University of Oregon, Center for the Advanced Study of Educational Administration.

Foster, W. (1991). <u>Moral theory, transformation, and leadership in school settings.</u> Paper presented at the annual meeting of the American Educational Research Association, Chicago.

Gibb, J. R. (1969). Dynamics of leadership. In F. D. Carver & T. J. Sergiovanni (Eds.), <u>Organizations and human behavior: Focus on the schools</u> (pp. 316-324). New York: McGraw-Hill.

Glasman, N. S. (1984). Student achievement and the principal. <u>Educational Evaluation and Policy Analysis, 6,</u> 55-68.

Glasman, N. S., & Nevo D. (1988). <u>Evaluation in decision making.</u> Boston: Kluwer Academic Publishers.

Glickman, C. D. (1990). Pushing school reform to a new edge: The seven ironies of school empowerment. <u>Phi Delta Kappan, 72,</u> 68-75.

Golembiewski, T. T., & McConkie, M. (1975). The centrality of interpersonal trust in group process. In C. L. Cooper (Ed.), <u>Theories of group process</u> (pp. 131-185). New York: John W. Wiley.

Gomez, D. (1987). <u>Principal influence on teacher behaviors: Perceptions from teachers and principals.</u> Unpublished doctoral dissertation, University of California, Santa Barbara.

Greenfield, W. D. (1982). <u>Empirical research on principals: The state of the art.</u> Paper presented at the annual meeting of the American Educational Research Association, New York.

Greenfield, W. D. (1987). <u>Moral imagination and value leadership in schools.</u> Paper presented at the annual meeting of the

American Educational Research Association, Washington, DC.

Halpin, A. W. (1966). <u>Theory and research in administration.</u> New York: MacMillan.

Harris, L. (1995). <u>Old problems, new challenges.</u> Survey conducted for Metropolitan Life Insurance. New York.

Heck, R. H., Larsen, T. J., & Marcoulides, G. A. (1990). Instructional leadership and school achievement: Validation of a causal model. <u>Educational Administration Quarterly, 26,</u> 94-125.

Henderson, J. E., & Hoy W. K. (1982). <u>Leader authenticity: The development and test of an operational measure.</u> Paper presented at the annual meeting of the American Educational Research Association, New York.

Hoy, W. K., & Kupersmith, W. J. (1985). The meaning and measure of faculty trust. <u>Educational and Psychological Research, 5,</u> 1-10.

Hoy, W. K., & Miskel, C. G. (1987). <u>Educational administration: Theory, research, and practice</u> (3rd. ed.). New York: Random House.

Hoy, W. K., Tarter, C. J., & Bliss, J. R. (1990). Organizational climate, school health, and effectiveness: A comparative analysis. <u>Educational Administration Quarterly, 26,</u> 260-279.

Hoy, W. K., Tarter, C. J., & Forsyth, P. (1978). Administrative behavior and subordinate loyalty: An empirical assessment. <u>Journal of Educational Administration. 16,</u> 29-38.

Hoy, W. K., Tarter, C. J., & Kottkamp, R. B. (1991). <u>Open schools/healthy schools: Measuring organizational climate.</u> Newbury Park, CA: Sage Publications.

Hughes, L. W. (1974). Achieving effective human relations and morale. In J. A. Culbertson, C. Henson, & R. Morrison. (Eds.). Performance objectives for principals: Concepts and instruments (pp. 112-151). Berkeley, CA: McCutchan.

Isherwood, G. B. (1973). The principal and his authority: An empirical study. High School Journal, 56(6), 291-303.

Johnson, N. A. (1984). The role of the Australian school principal in staff development. Unpublished Master's Thesis, University of New England, Armidale, New South Wales.

Johnston, G., & Venable, B. P. (1986). A study of teacher loyalty to the principal: Rule administration and hierarchical influence of the principal. Educational Administration Quarterly, 12, 4-27.

Kouzes, J. M., & Posner, B. Z. (1989). Leadership Practices Inventory. Palo Alto, CA: T. P. G. Learning Systems.

Kouzes, J. M., & Posner, B. Z. (1990). The leadership challenge: How to get extraordinary things done in organizations. San Francisco: Jossey-Bass.

Kozol, J. (1991). Savage inequalities: Children in America's schools. New York: Crown Publishers Inc.

Land, G., & Jarman, B. (1992). Breakpoint and beyond: Mastering the future today. New York: Harper Collins Publishers.

Larson, C. E., & LaFasto, F.M. (1989). TeamWork. Newbury Park, CA: Sage Publications.

Lee, V. E., Dedrick, R. F., & Smith, J. B. (1991). The effects of social organization on teachers' efficacy and satisfaction. Sociology of Education, 65, 190-208.

Leitner, D. (1994). Do principals affect student outcomes: An organizational perspective. School Effectiveness and School Improvement, 5,(3), 219-238.

Little, J. W. (1982). Norms of collegiality and experimentation: Workplace conditions of school success. American Educational Research Journal, 19, 325-340.

Mayo, H. (1945). The social problems of industrial civilization. Boston: Harvard University, Graduate School of Business Education.

McGregor, D. (1960). The human side of enterprise. New York: McGraw-Hill.

Miles, M. B. (1967). Some properties of schools as social systems. In G. Wanton (Ed.), Change in school systems. Washington, DC: National Training Laboratories, National Education Association.

Miles, M. B. (1969). Planned change and organizational health: figure and ground. In F. D. Carver & T. J. Sergiovanni (Eds.), Organizations and human behavior (pp. 375-391). New York: McGraw-Hill.

Moser, R. F. (1957). The leadership patterns of school superintendents and school principals. Administrator's Notebook. Chicago: Midwest Administration Center.

Muth, R. (1973). Teacher perceptions of power, conflict, and consensus. Administrator's Notebook. Chicago: Midwest Administration Center.

Ouchi, W. (1981, January 4). Theory Z: How American business can meet the Japanese challenge. New York Times Magazine, 42-45.

Parsons, T. (1961). An outline of the social system. In T. Parsons, E. Shils, K. Naegle, & J. Pitts (Eds.), Theories of society (pp. 30-79). New York: Free Press.

Parsons, T. (1967). Some ingredients of a general theory of formal organization. In A. W. Halpin (Ed.), Administrative theory in education (pp. 40-72). New York: Macmillan.

Paul, M. F. (1982). Power leadership and trust: Implications for counselors in terms of organizational change. Personnel and Guidance Journal, 60, 538-541.

Peterson, K. (1978). The principal's tasks. Administrator's Notebook, 28, 1-4.

Phi Delta Kappan. (1995, May).

Porter L. W., Steers, R. M., Mowday, R. T., & Boulian, P. V. (1974). 0rganizational commitment, job satisfaction, and turnover among psychiatric technicians. Journal of Applied Psychology, 59, 603-609.

Reitzug, U. C. (1989). Principal-teacher interactions in instructionally effective and ordinary elementary schools. Urban Education, 24, 38-58.

Rosenholtz, S. J. (1985). Effective schools: Interpreting the evidence. American Journal of Education, 93, 427-452.

Russell, J. S., Mazzarella, J. A., White, T., & Maurer, S. (1985). Linking the behaviors and activities of secondary school principals to effectiveness: A focus on effective and ineffective behaviors. Eugene: University of Oregon, Center of Educational Policy and Management.

Schmidt, M. L. (1994). Fact book: 1994-95. Sacramento: California Department of Education.

Selznick, P. (1957). <u>Leadership in administration: A sociological interpretation.</u> Evanston, IN: Row and Peterson.

Sergiovanni, T. J. (1984). Leadership and excellence in schooling. <u>Educational Leadership, 4</u>(5), 4-13.

Slater, M. R. (1991). <u>Leadership, social networks, and school performance.</u> Unpublished doctoral dissertation, University of California, Santa Barbara.

Sproul, L. (1981). Managing education programs: A micro-behavioral analysis. <u>Human Organization, 40</u>(2), 21-40.

Sullivan, J. B. (1988). <u>Team origins.</u> Denver: Performance Training Corp.

Tarter, C. J., Bliss, J., & Hoy, W. K. (1989). School characteristics and faculty trust in secondary schools. <u>Educational Administration Quarterly, 25,</u> 294-308.

Treslan, D. L., & Ryan, J. J. (1986). Perceptions of principals' influence bases. <u>The Canadian Administrator, 26</u>(2), 1-7.

Weber, M. (1930). <u>The protestant ethic and the spirit of capitalism.</u> New York: Scribner.

Weick, K. E. (1976). Educational organizations as loosely coupled systems. <u>Administrative Science Quarterly, 21,</u> 1-19.

Weiss, C. (1990). <u>How much shared leadership is there in public high schools?</u> Paper presented at the annual meeting of the American Educational Research Association, Boston.

Wilson, B., & Corbett, H. (1983). Organization and change: The effects of school linkages on the quality of implementation. <u>Educational Administration Quarterly, 19,</u> 85-104.

Wolcott, H. F. (1973). <u>The man in the principal's office: An ethnography.</u> New York: Holt, Rinehart, and Winston.

Wynne, E. A. (1980). <u>Looking at schools: Good, bad and indifferent.</u> Lexington, KY: D. C. Heath & Co.

APPENDIX A

Instructions for Questionnaires

Instructions for administration of questionnaires. To be read verbatim:

"Our school has been selected in a random sampling public schools in California to take part in a research project. In order to assist we have been asked to take a few minutes to fill out the following two questionnaires.

Frank DePasquale, a doctoral student at University of California, Santa Barbara and school administrator in Moorpark, California is collecting data for a dissertation. His topic centers around specific principal behaviors and how they relate to faculty trust.

All information collected will be confidential and there will be no way of tracking individual test scores. No school or individual will be identified by name in the final report. When the dissertation project is complete he will send us a summary of the results for our review.

Please take a few minutes to put an (X) over the line that describes your feelings about each statement. Please respond to each of the questions to the best of your ability. Do not put your name on any of the questionnaires. They are to be anonymous. When you have completed the questionnaires please return them to Mr./Ms./ Mrs. _____ who will place them in the envelope so as to maintain confidentiality.

Thank you again for your cooperation."

APPENDIX B

CLAS Statistical Report

NEWS RELEASE
CALIFORNIA DEPARTMENT OF EDUCATION

Contact: Susie Lange   (916) 657-3027   REL#94-49
                    FAX (916) 657-5101   EMBARGOED UNTIL
                                            06/03/94 a.m.

CLAS STATISTICAL REPORT RELEASED

SACRAMENTO—"The Select Committee on Sampling and
Statistical Procedures Used in the California Learning Assessment
System (CLAS) has now completed its work," said William D.
Dawson, Acting State Superintendent of Public Instruction. "I am
deeply grateful for the rigor of their thinking, and for their
diligence as they carried out their charge.

"As the Committee members noted, their work took them to the
very frontier of educational testing and measurement," continued
Dawson. "Their charge was to help us identify and solve problems
and they have done that with distinction. Their insights and
analyses will help us make significant progress in California's
student assessment and educational accountability program."

Due primarily to concerns about statistical errors on some
1993 CLAS school reports, Superintendent Dawson appointed the
three-member panel of nationally-recognized experts in the fields
of statistics and measurement in April. The panel was chaired by
Dr. Lee J. Cronbach of Stanford University, and included
Dr. Norman Bradburn of the University of Chicago and the National
Opinion Research Center and Dr. Daniel Horvitz of the National
Institute of Statistical Sciences. They were specifically charged
with reviewing the quality of the CLAS plan for sampling, scoring
and reporting school-level scores on the 1993 assessment; and
examining how well the contractors carried out that plan. In
addition, they were asked to evaluate the plan for analyzing and
reporting 1994 scores, including individual student results of
the 1994 assessment.

MORE...MORE...MORE

P.O. Box 944272 • Sacramento, California 94244-2720

94

REL#94-49
3-3-3-3

PROBLEM AREA #2: Technical Difficulties

All of the Committee's comments on test reliability rely on "standard error" (SE). As the Committee points out, the public encounters this concept in opinion polls when the results are described within a certain percent of accuracy. There is uncertainty in any measurement or survey, and the SE describes that uncertainty. The SE includes two kinds of error: sampling error and measurement error.

A.   Sampling Error

When the Committee began its deliberations there was widespread belief that the technical problems CLAS had encountered in its first year were related primarily to student sampling. (All students in a grade were tested, and a random sample of their papers was scored to compute the overall results for each school.) The Committee found that the CLAS sampling design was basically sound, however, the plan was poorly implemented in certain cases. In approximately three percent of the schools, the shortfall of papers scored was considered serious. This problem was initially identified by the Department and local school districts several months ago when it was found that a number of schools had erroneous school reports. Most of those reports have since been corrected.

Department Response:

The contractor has substantially improved its physical arrangements, equipment, record-keeping, and computer controls in order to prevent recurrence of the 1993 sampling shortfall.

The Department has also introduced sophisticated stratification procedures in the scoring plan which are expected to significantly reduce sampling error and increase the accuracy of the results for schools in 1994.

MORE...MORE...MORE

REL#94-49
5-5-5-5

Department Response:
Major changes have already been made in the measurement process in order to increase the accuracy and reliability of school and district reports for the 1994 and future assessment results. They include the following:

1. Strengthening the scoring process by:
   a. improving scorer training,
   b. raising the accuracy standards used to qualify scorers, and
   c. increasing the frequency and stringency of the procedures for monitoring scorer accuracy.
2. Formulating procedures for removing errors due to differences among assessment tasks and test forms.
3. Making additional improvements in the accuracy of the results for 1995 as a result of various studies that the Department and its contractors will conduct this summer and fall. The Committee report provided many extremely useful suggestions for such studies, including ways to identify and control various sources of error related to the scoring process.

C. Scores for Individual Students
   While the Committee found evidence of adequate reliability in pilot runs of the 1994 design for individual student scoring, they wanted greater assurance that the operational difficulties experienced in the 1993 school and district reporting would be remedied before attempting to report over 300,000 individual scores. They were also concerned that school personnel might use these results, without adequate corroborating information, to make important decisions that would affect students' lives, before sufficient study had been completed of the best means to interpret and use these new results. The Committee concluded

MORE...MORE...MORE

REL#94-49
7-7-7-7

A Final Note

"I urge everyone concerned about California's assessment system to read the entire report carefully," urged Dawson. "The Committee has met its charge and to our long term benefit has pulled no punches. There will, no doubt, continue to be calls to abandon our quest for performance-based assessment and return to the exclusively multiple choice format. Such pleas should be rejected. As the Committee points out in the executive summary:

> The legislation creating CLAS anticipated that development and implementation would be gradual, and that problem-solving over some years would be required to accomplish all the goals of the legislation. It is remarkable that CLAS has achieved so much by this time.

"CLAS has certainly experienced significant problems in the first two years," continued Dawson. "While some of those problems should have been anticipated, many others, as pointed out in this report, could not have been. That is the nature of such massive, bold, ground-breaking endeavors. There will be more new challenges as we move forward; but the goal -- a rigorous assessment system that requires students to actually demonstrate their ability to apply the skills and knowledge they have acquired in school, and that provides accountability for the results of our multi-billion dollar investment in education -- is vital. The Committee believes, and I fully agree, that this is not the time to lose our courage and turn back."

To order a copy of the full report, call (916) 657-3027. If you provide us with your express mail number, we will send it overnight. If you would like to pick up a copy of the report, you may come to Room 505 of the State Department of Education Building at 721 Capitol Mall, Sacramento. The 62 page document may also be sent first class mail, if you prefer.

# # # # #

APPENDIX C

Comparison Group of 100 Schools

```
CECOMP.OUT              April 6, 1994        Page 1

GRADE 6                                                              Page 1
                  54739606109867  ARROYO VEST ELEMENTA  MOORPARK UNIFIED 114


CDS NUM.          SCHOOL NAME          DISTRICT NAME

19647336016778    DIXIE CANYON AVENUE   LOS ANGELES UNIFIED  7
30736356094668    LOURDENA ELEMENTARY   SADDLEBACK VALLEY UN 127
19642126085617    CONSALVES ELEMENTARY  ABC UNIFIED 117
37683876040455    SKYLINE ELEMENTARY    SOLANA BEACH ELEMEN 145
19642616011191    LONGLEY WAY ELEMENTA  ARCADIA UNIFIED 13
62691956045647    FOOTHILL ELEMENTARY   GOLETA UNION ELEMEN 112
19642616011167    HIGHLAND OAKS ELEMEN  ARCADIA UNIFIED 108
19642126068276    CERRITOS ELEMENTARY   ABC UNIFIED 125
62691956045662    HOLLISTER ELEMENTARY  GOLETA UNION ELEMEN 101
19642126064716    STOWERS ELEMENTARY    ABC UNIFIED 145
19645686015742    LINCOLN (ABRAHAM) EL  GLENDALE UNIFIED 119
30666214071120    ROWL CANYON ELEMENTA  ORANGE UNIFIED 143
30736504089665    GREENTREE ELEMENTARY  IRVINE UNIFIED 159
19650604023105    BICKCRT ELEMENTARY    TORRANCE UNIFIED 145
27653916026418    MAGUIRE (EDNA) ELEME  MILL VALLEY ELEMENTA 141
19648326066773    OLD ORCHARD ELEMENTA  NEWHALL ELEMENTARY 45
37735516037790    MAGNOLIA ELEMENTARY   CARLSBAD UNIFIED 124
30736506100317    EASTSHORE ELEMENTARY  IRVINE UNIFIED 150
19648326029804    PEACHLAND AVENUE ELE  NEWHALL ELEMENTARY 132
30666214096333    IMPERIAL ELEMENTARY   ORANGE UNIFIED 127
19640076108922    RANCH HILLS ELEMENTA  POMONA UNIFIED 134
37620256038012    SUNNYSIDE ELEMENTARY  CHULA VISTA CITY 163
41690596046911    HIGHLANDS ELEMENTARY  SAN MATEO-FOSTER CIT 118
19736526022222    BLANDFORD ELEMENTARY  ROWLAND UNIFIED 105
36473146033013    COSUMNES ELEMENTARY   ELK GROVE UNIFIED 171
19647336020010    VANDERLAND AVENUE EL  LOS ANGELES UNIFIED
30736356071153    DEL CERRO ELEMENTARY  SADDLEBACK VALLEY UN 165
30736506100661    NORTHWOOD ELEMENTARY  IRVINE UNIFIED 136
49706236051601    NENNETT VALLEY ELEME  NENNETT VALLEY UNION 146
61689736044250    SPRING VALLEY ELEMEN  MILLBRAE ELEMENTARY 95
37682966106520    CANYON VIEW ELEMENTA  POWAY UNIFIED 145
61689736044236    MEADOWS ELEMENTARY    MILLBRAE ELEMENTARY 141
63696616048359    PALO VERDE ELEMENTAR  PALO ALTO UNIFIED
30736356030159    LINDA VISTA ELEMENTA  SADDLEBACK VALLEY UN 110
19645686015843    DUNSMORE ELEMENTARY   GLENDALE UNIFIED 125
19650276022768    ARROYO VISTA ELEMENT  SOUTH PASADENA UNIFI 137
19643946012157    CHAPARRAL ELEMENTARY  CLAREMONT UNIFIED 149
19642126093647    VITTMANN ELEMENTARY   ABC UNIFIED 177
62592116045553    VIEJA VALLEY ELEMENT  HOPE ELEMENTARY 146
63694356102081    NORWOOD CREEK ELEMEN  EVERGREEN ELEMENTARY 111
19450606023238    SEASIDE ELEMENTARY    TORRANCE UNIFIED 156
30665976029336    RANGOR VIEW ELEMENTA  NEWPORT-MESA UNIFIED 180
37680236095020    TIFFANY (BURTON C.)   CHULA VISTA CITY 179
30736356046866    MISO ELEMENTARY       SADDLEBACK VALLEY UN 137
19642126085609    LEAL ELEMENTARY       ABC UNIFIED 113
19642126093654    NIXON ELEMENTARY      ABC UNIFIED 140
30736356030530    TRABUCO ELEMENTARY    SADDLEBACK VALLEY UN 144
64497996049738    RAM VISTA ELEMENTARY  PAJARO VALLEY JOINT 94
30665066028153    ROLLING HILLS ELEMEN  FULLERTON ELEMENTARY 97
36476786035554    GLENMEADE ELEMENTARY  CHINO UNIFIED 100
30665226028369    ALLEN (ETHAN B.) ELE  GARDEN GROVE UNIFIED 104
```

Dr. Frank DePasquale

GCCOMP.OUT   April 6, 1994   Page 6

GRADE 6   Page 2
                 56739406109647 ARROYO WEST ELEMENTA MOORPARK UNIFIED

    CDS NUM.   SCHOOL NAME   DISTRICT NAME

30739246029045   HOPKINSON (FRANCIS) LOS ALAMITOS UNIFIED 129
30666216029862   LAVETA ELEMENTARY ORANGE UNIFIED 140
30664646098695   YANKEY (CARL N.) ELE CAPISTRANO UNIFIED 130
30666216029938   SERRANO ELEMENTARY ORANGE UNIFIED 137
30666646027593   CROWN VALLEY ELEMENT CAPISTRANO UNIFIED 134
37482966110878   ADOBE BLUFFS ELEMENT POWAY UNIFIED 156
43676616048409   HAYS (WALTER) ELEMEN PALO ALTO UNIFIED 189
56737576055842   ACACIA ELEMENTARY CONEJO VALLEY UNIFIE 135
36676786106611   LITEL (GERALD F.) EL CHINO UNIFIED 99
30736356094676   SAN JOAQUIN ELEMENTA SADDLEBACK VALLEY UN 97
42591956065421   ELLWOOD ELEMENTARY GOLETA UNION ELEMENT 93
43675836098271   PARADISE VALLEY ELEM MORGAN HILL UNIFIED 61
37636526040638   MONTE VISTA ELEMENTA VISTA UNIFIED 177
54725536055404   DOS CAMINOS ELEMENTA PLEASANT VALLEY ELEM 70
57726736110894   PATWIN ELEMENTARY DAVIS JOINT UNIFIED 141
19647336018618   OVERLAND AVENUE ELEM LOS ANGELES UNIFIED
19647256015457   LONGFELLOW ELEMENTAR LONG BEACH UNIFIED 107
27660926026322   MONTE VISTA ELEMENTA MONTEREY PENINSULA U 140
19642206011001   BRIGHTWOOD ELEMENTAR ALHAMBRA CITY ELEMEN 121
49703476051908   SERRANO ELDREDGE ELE OLD ADOBE UNION ELEM 97
44697996049720   LINSCOTT (J. W.) ELE PAJARO VALLEY JOINT 72
41690136044630   CRESTMOOR ELEMENTARY SAN BRUNO PARK ELEME 109
13631236008660   MEDRICK (MARGARET) E EL CENTRO ELEMENTARY 66
56726526056121   LOMA VISTA ELEMENTAR VENTURA UNIFIED 95
41690396044895   FOSTER CITY ELEMENTA SAN MATEO-FOSTER CIT 118
07617966097141   HERCULES ELEMENTARY RICHMOND UNIFIED 115
37680236038038   VALLEY VISTA ELEMENT CHULA VISTA CITY 146
43694196047088   STEVENS CREEK ELEMEN CUPERTINO UNION ELEM 157
30664806027841   MORRIS (JULIET) ELEM CYPRESS ELEMENTARY 104
30736506096192   WESTWOOD BASICS PLUS IRVINE UNIFIED 142
43695266047542   LOUISE VAN METER ELE LOS GATOS UNION ELEM 126
37682966099444   SUNDANCE ELEMENTARY POWAY UNIFIED 143
30736356030183   GATES (RALPH A.) ELE SADDLEBACK VALLEY UN 118
19649076101133   DECKER ELEMENTARY ROMONA UNIFIED 99
30666136029540   CIRCLE VIEW ELEMENTA OCEAN VIEW ELEMENTAR 162
10621176005862   FORT WASHINGTON ELEM CLOVIS UNIFIED 130
30666646106801   SERGESON (MARIAN) EL CAPISTRANO UNIFIED 119
30665976029359   KAISER (HEINZ) ELEME NEWPORT-MESA UNIFIED 100
30666216107767   CHAPMAN HILLS ELEMEN ORANGE UNIFIED 145
43693776067177   RUSKIN ELEMENTARY BERRYESSA UNION ELEN 116
30664646108740   WHITE (GEORGE) ELEME CAPISTRANO UNIFIED —
19643296011845   LAVERNE HEIGHTS ELEM BONITA UNIFIED 125
19734606023378   EVERGREEN ELEMENTARY WALNUT VALLEY UNIFIE 169
42591956065504   MOUNTAIN VIEW ELEMEN GOLETA UNION ELEMENT 177
33672156032783   WASHINGTON ELEMENTAR RIVERSIDE UNIFIED 72
19650606023279   TOWERS ELEMENTARY TORRANCE UNIFIED 108
19647666020176   MACY ELEMENTARY (RSP LOWELL JOINT ELEMENT 127
33670586109045   MONROE (JAMES) ELEME DESERT SANDS UNIFIED 72
30664646095087   MOULTON ELEMENTARY CAPISTRANO UNIFIED 131

100

APPENDIX D

Type I and Type II Schools

TYPE I SCHOOLS

150 (+)

Walter Hays Elementary School (K-5 - 270)   I.D. # 101
1525 Middlefield Road
Palo Alto, CA 94302   Score 139
(415) 322-5956
Harold Jones, Principal

Harbor View Elementary School (1-6 - 751)   I.D. # 102
900 Goldenrod Avenue
Corona del Mar, CA 92525   Score 180
(714) 760-3472
Paul Twedt, Principal

Mountain View Elementary School (K-6 - 434)   I.D. # 103
5465 Queen Ann Lane
Santa Barbara, CA 93111   Score 176
(805) 681-1284
JoAnne Meade Young, Principal

Helen Wittmann Elementary School (K-6 - 512)   I.D. # 104
16801 Yverre Avenue
Cerritos, CA 90701   Score 177
(310) 926-1321
Wade Austin, Principal

Cosumnes River Elementary School (K-6 - 219)   I.D. # 105
13580 Jackson Road
Sloughhouse, CA 95683   Score 171
(916) 682-2653
Judy Hunt, Principal

Evergreen Elementary School (K-5 - 750)   I.D. # 106
1450 S. Evergreen Springs Road
Diamond Bar, CA 91765   Score 169
(909) 594-1041
Albert Stone, Principal

Highland Oaks Elementary School (K-6 - 682)   I.D. # 107
Ten Virginia Drive
Arcadia, CA 91006   Score 168
(818) 446-3155
Michael M. Simoniello, Principal

Del Cerro Elementary School (K-6 - 481)   I.D. # 108
24382 Regina Street
Mission Viejo, CA 92691   Score 165
(714) 830-5430
Suzanne Westmoreland, Principal

Circle View Elementary School (K-5 - 635)   I.D. # 109
6261 Hooker Street
Huntington Beach, CA 92647   Score 142
Dan Moss, Principal

Joe A. Gonsalves Elementary School (K-6 - 550)   I.D. # 110
13650 Park Street
Cerritos, CA 90701   Score 157
(310) 926-1347
Decla Johnson, Principal

Adobe Bluffs Elementary School (K-5 - 423)   I.D. # 111
8707 Adobe Bluffs Drive
San Diego, CA 92127   Score 156
(619) 538-8403
Diane Cantelli, Principal

Seaside Elementary School (K-5 - 457)   I.D. # 112
4651 Sharynne Lane
Torrance, CA 90505   Score 156
(310) 533-4532
Jeanne Gelwicks, Principal

Eastshore Elementary School (K-6 510)   I.D. # 113
155 Eastshore
Irvine, CA 92714   Score 150
(714) 552-7228
Susanne Wiegand, Principal

TYPE II SCHOOLS

95 (-)

Paradise Valley Elementary School (K-6 - 765)
1400 La Crosse Drive
Morgan Hill, CA 95037
(408) 779-8391
Brendan White, Principal

I.D. # 114

Score 61

Margaret Hedrick Elementary School (K-6 - 671)
550 S. Waterman Avenue
El Centro, CA 92243
(619) 352-4750
Byron Isaac, Principal

I.D. # 115

Score 66

Dos Caminos School K-6 - 443)
3635 Appian Way
Camarillo, CA 93010-4099
(805) 482-9894
Barbara Wagner, Principal

I.D. # 116

Score 70

Overland Elementary School (K-6 - 495)
10650 Ashby Avenue
Los Angeles, CA 90064
(310) 838-7308
Suzanne DiJulio, Principal

I.D. # 117

Score 76

Dixie Canyon Elementary School (K-6 - 763)
4220 Dixie Canyon Avenue
Sherman Oaks, CA 91423
(818) 784-6283
Melanie Ann Deutsch, Principal

I.D. # 118

Score 76

San Joaquin Elementary School (K-6 - 625)
22182 Barbera
Laguna Hills, CA 92653
(714) 581-3450
Kathy Wright, Principal

I.D. # 119

Score 97

Decker Elementary School (K-6 - 828)
20 Village Loop Road
Pomona, CA 91766
(909) 397-4582
Virginia B. Scott, Principal

I.D. # 120

Score 94

Mar Vista Elementary School (K-6 - 500)
6860 Soquel Drive
P.O. Box 100
Aptos, CA 95003
(408) 688-5211
Barry Marks, Principal

I.D. # 121

Score 94

Old Orchard Elementary School (K-6 - 770)   I.D. # 122
25141 N. Avenida Rondel
Valencia, CA 91355   Score 95
(805) 286-2284
Betty Granger, Principal

Spring Valley Elementary School (K-5 - 368)   I.D. # 123
817 Murchison Drive
Millbrae, CA 94030   Score 95
(415) 697-5681
Sharon DeBiagio, Principal

Loma Vista Elementary School (K-5 - 333)   I.D. # 124
300 Lynn Drive
Ventura, CA 93003   Score 95
(805) 643-5444
Richard Kirby, Principal

APPENDIX E

Principal Behavior Scale

PRINCIPAL BEHAVIOR SCALE

1. Teachers in this school receive letters and notes praising their action, from the principal.

    Strongly Agree   Strongly Disagree

    | 6 | 5 | 4 | 3 | 2 | 1 |

2. Teachers in this school feel that the principal tries to protect their instructional time.

    Strongly Agree   Strongly Disagree

    | 6 | 5 | 4 | 3 | 2 | 1 |

3. Teachers in this school are consulted on decisions that affect what happens in their classrooms.

    Strongly Agree   Strongly Disagree

    | 6 | 5 | 4 | 3 | 2 | 1 |

4. Teachers in this school feel that the principal shows genuine concern about their personal lives.

    Strongly Agree   Strongly Disagree

    | 6 | 5 | 4 | 3 | 2 | 1 |

5. Teachers in this school are recognized at award ceremonies.

    Strongly Agree   Strongly Disagree

    | 6 | 5 | 4 | 3 | 2 | 1 |

6. Teachers in this school feel that the principal defends them against unwarranted parent complaints.

Strongly Agree   Strongly Disagree

| 6 | 5 | 4 | 3 | 2 | 1 |

7. Teachers and parents meet with the principal on a routine basis to assist in site level decision making.

Strongly Agree   Strongly Disagree

| 6 | 5 | 4 | 3 | 2 | 1 |

8. Teachers in this school feel that the principal shows genuine concern about their professional growth.

Strongly Agree   Strongly Disagree

| 6 | 5 | 4 | 3 | 2 | 1 |

9. Teachers in this school receive verbal praise and encouragement from the principal.

Strongly Agree   Strongly Disagree

| 6 | 5 | 4 | 3 | 2 | 1 |

10. Teachers in this school feel that the principal handles student discipline in a manner that reflects support of teachers.

Strongly Agree   Strongly Disagree

| 6 | 5 | 4 | 3 | 2 | 1 |

11. When the principal asks for advice from teachers, it is taken seriously and acted upon.

Strongly Agree   Strongly Disagree

_____   _____   _____   _____   _____   _____
     6   5   4   3   2   1

12. Teachers in this school try new ideas and programs.

Strongly Agree   Strongly Disagree

_____   _____   _____   _____   _____   _____
     6   5   4   3   2   1

13. Teachers in this school receive nonverbal praise such as smiles, handshakes and pats on the back, from the principal.

Strongly Agree   Strongly Disagree

_____   _____   _____   _____   _____   _____
     6   5   4   3   2   1

14 Teachers in this school feel that their meetings are productive.

Strongly Agree   Strongly Disagree

_____   _____   _____   _____   _____   _____
     6   5   4   3   2   1

15. Teachers in this school are given a wide range of responsibilities by the principal.

Strongly Agree   Strongly Disagree

_____   _____   _____   _____   _____   _____
     6   5   4   3   2   1

16   Teachers in this school feel that the principal shows a genuine interest regarding their family members.

Strongly Agree   Strongly Disagree

| 6 | 5 | 4 | 3 | 2 | 1 |

17. Teachers in this school feel that praise for their teaching is an important aspect related to their job satisfaction.

Strongly Agree   Strongly Disagree

| 6 | 5 | 4 | 3 | 2 | 1 |

18   Teachers in this school feel that they are asked to do a fair amount of paper work.

Strongly Agree   Strongly Disagree

| 6 | 5 | 4 | 3 | 2 | 1 |

19   Teachers who are involved in making site level decisions with the principal feel that their time is being used productively, and that they do have an impact on the final decision.

Strongly Agree   Strongly Disagree

| 6 | 5 | 4 | 3 | 2 | 1 |

20   The principal really cares about the general well being of the entire staff.

Strongly Agree   Strongly Disagree

| 6 | 5 | 4 | 3 | 2 | 1 |

APPENDIX F

Trust in Principal Scale

TRUST IN PRINCIPAL SCALE

1. The teachers in this school are suspicious of most of the principal's actions.

    Strongly Agree   Strongly Disagree

    | 1 | 2 | 3 | 4 | 5 | 6 |

2. The teachers in this school have faith in the integrity of the principal.

    Strongly Agree   Strongly Disagree

    | 6 | 5 | 4 | 3 | 2 | 1 |

3. The principal takes unfair advantage of the teachers in this school.

    Strongly Agree   Strongly Disagree

    | 1 | 2 | 3 | 4 | 5 | 6 |

4   The principal in this school typically acts with the best interests of the teachers in mind.

    Strongly Agree   Strongly Disagree

    | 6 | 5 | 4 | 3 | 2 | 1 |

5   Teachers in this school often question the motives of the principal.

    Strongly Agree   Strongly Disagree

    | 1 | 2 | 3 | 4 | 5 | 6 |

6. Teachers in this school trust the principal.

    Strongly Agree   Strongly Disagree

    | 6 | 5 | 4 | 3 | 2 | 1 |

7   The principal in this school keeps his/her word.

    Strongly Agree   Strongly Disagree

    | 6 | 5 | 4 | 3 | 2 | 1 |

APPENDIX G

Scores for Schools

TOTAL OBSERVATIONS 18 SCHOOLS

	B1	B2	B3	B4	B5
N OF CASES	269	269	268	268	262
MINIMUM	1.000	1.000	1.000	1.000	1.000
MAXIMUM	6.000	6.000	6.000	6.000	6.000
RANGE	5.000	5.000	5.000	5.000	5.000
MEAN	4.338	5.104	4.955	4.746	3.714
STANDARD DEV	1.425	1.070	1.170	1.358	1.658

	B6	B7	B8	B9	B10
N OF CASES	263	265	265	263	264
MINIMUM	1.000	1.000	1.000	1.000	1.000
MAXIMUM	6.000	6.000	6.000	6.000	6.000
RANGE	5.000	5.000	5.000	5.000	5.000
MEAN	5.125	4.958	5.166	4.878	5.038
STANDARD DEV	1.141	1.222	1.031	1.263	1.211

	B11	B12	B13	B14	B15
N OF CASES	265	267	266	267	267
MINIMUM	2.000	2.000	1.000	1.000	2.000
MAXIMUM	6.000	6.000	6.000	6.000	6.000
RANGE	4.000	4.000	5.000	5.000	4.000
MEAN	5.045	5.255	4.947	4.644	5.199
STANDARD DEV	0.968	0.971	1.098	1.184	0.885

	B16	B17	B18	B19	B20
N OF CASES	254	259	257	257	260
MINIMUM	1.000	1.000	1.000	1.000	2.000
MAXIMUM	6.000	6.000	6.000	6.000	6.000
RANGE	5.000	5.000	5.000	5.000	4.000
MEAN	4.441	4.992	4.416	4.926	5.300
STANDARD DEV	1.412	1.151	1.415	1.064	0.948

	T1	T2	T3	T4	T5
N OF CASES	268	268	268	267	268
MINIMUM	1.000	1.000	1.000	1.000	1.000
MAXIMUM	6.000	6.000	6.000	6.000	6.000
RANGE	5.000	5.000	5.000	5.000	5.000
MEAN	5.399	5.373	5.396	5.247	4.854
STANDARD DEV	1.043	1.025	1.035	1.082	1.244

	T6	T7
N OF CASES	268	268
MINIMUM	2.000	1.000
MAXIMUM	6.000	6.000
RANGE	4.000	5.000
MEAN	5.295	5.373
STANDARD DEV	0.971	0.863

SCHOOL TYPE I

TOTAL OBSERVATIONS   9 SCHOOLS

	B1	B2	B3	B4	B5
N OF CASES	128	128	127	127	124
MINIMUM	1.000	2.000	2.000	1.000	1.000
MAXIMUM	6.000	6.000	6.000	6.000	6.000
MEAN	4.430	5.266	5.094	4.858	3.806
STANDARD DEV	1.494	0.960	1.003	1.213	1.733

	B6	B7	B8	B9	B10
N OF CASES	124	125	125	124	125
MINIMUM	1.000	1.000	1.000	2.000	1.000
MAXIMUM	6.000	6.000	6.000	6.000	6.000
MEAN	5.185	5.080	5.256	4.968	4.968
STANDARD DEV	1.054	1.126	0.991	1.189	1.307

	B11	B12	B13	B14	B15
N OF CASES	126	126	125	126	126
MINIMUM	2.000	2.000	2.000	1.000	3.000
MAXIMUM	6.000	6.000	6.000	6.000	6.000
MEAN	5.214	5.476	5.120	4.635	5.294
STANDARD DEV	0.806	0.712	0.930	1.107	0.749

	B16	B17	B18	B19	B20
N OF CASES	122	124	124	123	125
MINIMUM	1.000	2.000	1.000	2.000	2.000
MAXIMUM	6.000	6.000	6.000	6.000	6.000
MEAN	4.443	5.145	4.524	4.976	5.472
STANDARD DEV	1.361	0.943	1.284	0.962	0.789

	T1	T2	T3	T4	T5
N OF CASES	128	128	128	127	128
MINIMUM	1.000	1.000	2.000	2.000	1.000
MAXIMUM	6.000	6.000	6.000	6.000	6.000
MEAN	5.523	5.445	5.508	5.339	4.922
STANDARD DEV	0.896	1.048	0.905	1.017	1.277

	T6	T7
N OF CASES	128	128
MINIMUM	2.000	2.000
MAXIMUM	6.000	6.000
MEAN	5.352	5.375
STANDARD DEV	0.884	0.832

SCHOOL TYPE II

TOTAL OBSERVATIONS   9 SCHOOLS

	B1	B2	B3	B4	B5
N OF CASES	141	141	141	141	138
MINIMUM	1.000	1.000	1.000	1.000	1.000
MAXIMUM	6.000	6.000	6.000	6.000	6.000
MEAN	4.255	4.957	4.830	4.645	3.630
STANDARD DEV	1.360	1.146	1.293	1.474	1.590

	B6	B7	B8	B9	B10
N OF CASES	139	140	140	139	139
MINIMUM	1.000	1.000	1.000	1.000	1.000
MAXIMUM	6.000	6.000	6.000	6.000	6.000
MEAN	5.072	4.850	5.086	4.799	5.101
STANDARD DEV	1.214	1.297	1.063	1.325	1.118

	B11	B12	B13	B14	B15
N OF CASES	139	141	141	141	141
MINIMUM	2.000	2.000	1.000	1.000	2.000
MAXIMUM	6.000	6.000	6.000	6.000	6.000
MEAN	4.892	5.057	4.794	4.652	5.113
STANDARD DEV	1.075	1.120	1.210	1.253	0.986

	B16	B17	B18	B19	B20
N OF CASES	132	135	133	134	135
MINIMUM	1.000	1.000	1.000	1.000	2.000
MAXIMUM	6.000	6.000	6.000	6.000	6.000
MEAN	4.439	4.852	4.316	4.881	5.141
STANDARD DEV	1.463	1.302	1.524	1.151	1.052

	T1	T2	T3	T4	T5
N OF CASES	140	140	140	140	140
MINIMUM	1.000	1.000	1.000	1.000	1.000
MAXIMUM	6.000	6.000	6.000	6.000	6.000
MEAN	5.286	5.307	5.293	5.164	4.793
STANDARD DEV	1.152	1.003	1.135	1.136	1.214

	T6	T7
N OF CASES	140	140
MINIMUM	2.000	1.000
MAXIMUM	6.000	6.000
MEAN	5.243	5.371
STANDARD DEV	1.045	0.892